THE ADMINISTRATION OF THE ROMAN EMPIRE (241BC–AD193)

Edited by

David C. Braund

UNIVERSITY
of
EXETER
PRESS

ISBN: 1469164

First published by the University of Exeter Press in 1988.
Reprinted 1993.

University of Exeter Press
Reed Hall
Streatham Drive
Exeter EX4 4QR
UK

DG
83
. A351
1988

British Library Cataloguing in Publication Data

A catalogue record of this book is available from the British Library

ISBN 0 85989 204 2
ISSN 0260 8628

Printed in Great Britain by Short Run Press Ltd, Exeter

Contents

Preface

The purpose of this book is to offer a concise account of principal features of the administration of the Roman empire from the end of the First Punic War in 241 BC to the accession of Septimius Severus in AD 193. A particular effort has been made to incorporate recent discoveries and new ideas, though a complete coverage of every aspect of the subject has never been feasible in a work of this scale. It is hoped that this little book may prove useful to a wide range of readers, but the needs of the undergraduate and diligent sixth-former have been the main priority.

I would very much like to thank my fellow-contributors for their endeavour, assistance and patience. I am also grateful to Dr Colin Jones and to my wife for their help with the trials and technicalities of production. And I am indebted to Dr Malyn Newitt for acute proof-reading. Mike Rouillard designed the cover.

List of Figures

Introduction:

the Growth of the Roman Empire

(241BC–AD193)

David C. Braund

Administration can function in many different ways. Much changed in
Rome and her empire from 241 BC to AD 193, including the manner of
Rome's imperial administration, yet throughout this period the very essence
of that administration continued to be local self-administration. To a great
extent, local communities, local elites and local rulers continued to man-
age their own affairs with relatively little interference from the centre of
power at Rome or from Roman officials (though see Reynolds in this volume on *curatores*). And, in general, these local administrations continued
to operate in accordance with local traditions—even, to some extent, where
Roman interference and Roman impact were most profound, as in much of
the West (Drinkwater 1983, 93ff.; cf.Hanson in this volume). For the most
part, Rome was willing to tolerate the wide variety of local structures and
practices which existed within her empire, provided that they did not conflict substantially with her twin priorities—the maintenance of order in the
broadest sense and the collection of taxes.

Previous studies of Roman imperial administration have certainly acknowledged this simple truth, but often they have also tended to focus
attention upon Roman governors at the expense of local peoples, cities and
kings. The focus of this volume is different: local structures and practices
take pride of place and Roman governors are discussed essentially in relation to them, not vice-versa. The main purpose of this brief introduction is
to present recent advances in our understanding of the activities of Roman
governors and give references to the more useful and accessible modern
discussions of their role.

It has often been observed that Rome was ill-equipped for the empire which Roman military success created. Certainly, Rome was still a city-state at the end of the First Punic War (264–241 BC). Upon her victory in that war, she acquired her first overseas commitment—Western Sicily. Our inadequate information might suggest that Rome found it difficult to settle upon the best means of controlling this area. Earlier Roman expansion in Italy had generated no necessary precedent (cf.North 1981). Meanwhile, the eastern part of the island was left to the rule of Rome's ally King Hiero of Sicily, who is sometimes considered by modern scholars to have been Rome's first 'client king' (Eckstein 1980 provides a useful biography; cf.Braund in this volume). Rome soon acquired Sardinia and Corsica and, as a result of the Second Punic War, much of the huge Spanish peninsula. The Roman city-state had to find some acceptable and practical means of dealing with these growing commitments. Local self-administration provided a large part of the means, but this had to be co-ordinated: local order had first to be established and enemies had to be dealt with (whether real, imagined or created: cf.Harris 1979). A major stimulus to the creation of a province was the Roman need or wish to wage war—provinces were not created because of some Roman need or wish to take on administration for its own sake. Richardson acutely observes, particularly with reference to the 'annexation' of Spain:

> The assignment of a *provincia* marked out an area of military responsibility, and as such was not an act of annexation but an act of war...it may be seen that what the Romans were doing in Spain was essentially the same as what they were doing in the Greek east, that is using all means available to ensure that the peoples of the Mediterranean did what the Romans wanted them to do. (Richardson 1986, 178-9).

War, of course, included action against pirates, who were a serious problem for Republican Rome in particular: the Roman need to take such action seems to have been the main reason for the annexation of Cyrene, probably in 75 BC, though that case also indicates the plurality of special local circumstances which doubtless obtained in the creation of any province (Braund 1985).

The Roman city-state had a number of magistrates—notably, consuls, praetors and, at a more junior level, quaestors—who might be sent out to co-ordinate administration as far as was necessary. Above all, consuls and praetors might be sent out to sustain warfare as the commanders of armies (which comprised substantial non-Roman forces as well as Roman legions: Keppie 1984 provides an excellent account of the development of the Roman army). Moreover, it was traditional that consuls and praetors should lead Rome's armies and dispense justice, while quaestors regularly dealt with implications of finance and supply, often as the assistants of consuls and praetors. In one sense it was therefore an obvious step to send these magistrates overseas to take on Rome's new commitments, particularly to wage war. But that step also involved significant difficulties. The most important difficulty was that there were only a few such magistrates—in 241 BC there were two consuls, two praetors (one of whom, the so-called peregrine praetor, had just been created to deal with judicial matters involving foreigners, *peregrini*) and perhaps eight quaestors; these were insufficient to cope with the growing empire.

Innovations were evidently desirable, but the overwhelming Roman concern for tradition tended to restrict their scope. An increase in the number of consuls would probably have been considered too great a break with tradition and too socially and politically unsettling. The number of praetors was increased from two to four about 227 BC to deal with western Sicily and Sardinia. In 198 BC the number of praetors was again increased to cope with Spain, which was deemed to require two such magistrates, each with his own *provincia*. There were now six praetors (though the innovation was not entirely secure at first: see Sherwin-White 1984, 8-9): Sulla increased their number to eight. The number of quaestors may also have been increased before Sulla eventually made their number twenty. In principle, these magistrates were elected for one year of office. A further means of increasing the number of magistrates was to extend their tenure of office, under a title which indicated the extension—a consul might be made a proconsul, a praetor a propraetor. Extension of office (*prorogatio*), though used earlier in Italy (Livy 8.26.7), became significantly more common in the course of the second century BC.

Imperialism was stretching and changing the superstructure of the Roman city-state. Another symptom was the creation of the first standing court at Rome in 149 BC: though much remains uncertain, it is clear enough that this court was in some sense a by-product of imperialism, set up to deal with the malpractice of Roman magistrates in the provinces (Richardson 1986, 137-40; 1987). Roman citizens active overseas needed some protection from the possibly arbitrary decisions of such magistrates. Moreover, bad behaviour by magistrates was a threat to local order. At the same time, Romans, like many other imperialists, often liked to see themselves as exercising a beneficent rule over those who made up their empire (Brunt 1978; Nutton 1978). However, the ultimate inadequacy of Roman concern for non-Roman victims of magistrates in the provinces— however loudly and powerfully that concern might be declared— is indicated by recurrent (though not total) failure to prosecute and to convict the guilty (Richardson 1986, 140). Concern for provincials was often conditional upon the exigencies of power-politics within the elite at Rome itself. Imperialism had set the political struggles of that elite on a larger stage and had set its conflicts in a new context. In addition to political ideology and practice, imperialism also changed social and economic structures, as the Republic, largely as a result of imperialism, became the Principate (see Braund 1987 and the literature there cited).

The change in meaning of the term *provincia* is a further symptom of the impact of the success of Roman imperialism upon Rome itself. Richardson has recently shown the full inadequacy of the usual translation, 'province', especially in the early period of Roman imperialism (Richardson 1986, 4-7). Originally —and, to an extent, always thereafter—*provincia* denoted a magistrate's task. That task might have a geographical prescription, but need not—for example, a *provincia* could be a war or a judicial function. By the Late Republic, however, the term had come to denote primarily a certain sort of geographical area in which a magistrate exercised a certain sort of function. A province was now a recognisable entity and an organic part of the Roman state. The evolution in meaning of the term *provincia* corresponds to the emergence of the Roman city-state as a world-empire, for, as Romans saw, that is what Rome increasingly became, especially after the work of Augustus.

By the time of Cicero's governorship in Cilicia in 51-50 BC, *provincia* was taken to refer most naturally to a geographical area whose boundaries were usually (though not always) defined and which functioned according to a few very broad norms (Lintott 1981, 54). Over the years a succession of Roman magistrates had established in each of 'the provinces' (as they were by now regularly called) a set of legal regulations and practices which were passed on, with occasional emendations, from each magistrate to his successor. Boards of commissioners, despatched by the Senate, regularly played a significant part in framing these bodies of law, especially in the early days of Roman involvement in an area, but the scope and importance of their activities should not be over-estimated and the role of individual magistrates neglected (Lintott 1981, 59-61; Richardson 1986, 165). In particular, the Roman magistrate was, despite such commissioners, in a position of huge personal power. The only formal limitation upon him was the possibility of his prosecution at the end of his tenure of office. Cicero's letters from his province provide ample illustrations of the magistrate's freedom of action as provincial governor, not only in Cicero's own behaviour but also in that of his predecessor (Treggiari 1972 offers a convenient selection and commentary).

It is entirely probable that Cicero's speeches against Verres and others contain much that is exaggerated and misleading (perhaps more than is often imagined), but they do make very clear the overwhelming power of a Roman provincial governor under the Republic. Yet there also existed extra-legal checks upon him. Cicero's letters from Cilicia harp upon his concern for his reputation (*fama*) as a good governor. This was no doubt particularly important to Cicero, who had said and written so much on the subject of good government, but there is no reason to suppose his concern for his reputation to be a personal quirk - quite the contrary, in fact (Braund 1988; cf. Wiseman 1985b). Cicero sums up his governorship thus:

> As for everything else [i.e.other than arrangements for his departure from Cilicia], so far there's nothing but praise and gratitude worthy of the books of which you speak so highly [i.e.Cicero's *On the Republic*; cf.*ad Att.*6.2.9]. I have rescued the communities and have more than satisfied the tax-farmers. I have offended nobody by insulting behaviour. I have offended a very few by just, stern decisions, but never so much that they have the audacity to complain. I have achieved military successes which deserve a triumph... (Cicero *ad Att.*6.3.3).

The prime concerns of the Republican governor are clearly set out and Cicero's concern for his good name is evident. Military success and, if possible, the crowning glory of a triumphal procession through Rome were major goals for a member of the Roman elite (Versnel 1970; Wiseman 1985b). At the very least, the governor was expected to deal with bandits and pirates as far as lay within his power: hence Cicero's denunciation of Verres for not only failing to do this, but actually helping pirates (Cic.*In Verr.* 2.5.11, for example). However, Cicero was hardly less concerned with the potential conflicts between himself, provincial communities and Roman tax-farmers (*publicani*). He expresses particular relief that the most contentious part of the tax-farmers' work in his province had been completed before his arrival to take up his post (*ad Att.*5.13). Exploitation by tax-farmers was a constant threat to local stability and order—yet governors seem regularly to have connived at it, if only to avoid the consequences of a clash with the powerful *publicani* and the private interests at Rome in which they acted. This was the price which the Roman Republic paid for raising public revenues through private organisations (on which, see Badian 1972). The activities of Roman debt-collectors outside Italy could also be very damaging, especially when they were abetted by Roman governors (e.g.*ad Att.*6.1.6).

Yet another problem for the governor was the dispensing of justice which was a major part of his task (Burton 1975)— Cicero hints at the difficulties of being judge and staying popular. Unpopularity with the powerful and the possibility of social isolation and even prosecution might be forestalled by the respectful personal conduct and controlled use of power upon which he prides himself. He had passed the test of governorship (a *discrimen: ad Att.*5.13.1).

Cicero's long letter to his brother on the subject of proper governorship (*ad Q.fr.*1.1) presents a similar ideology of governorship in more expanded form. Of particular interest is the extent to which Cicero regards Greek political theory on monarchy as relevant to the Roman governor in practice: he advises his brother to read Xenophon's *Cyropaedia* as Scipio Aemilianus had done in the second century BC. The autocratic position of the governor did indeed have something in common with that of a king, though, of course, the governor's tenure of office was limited, unlike that of a king, and he might be brought to book. In Cicero's view, the good Roman governor, like the good king, must exercise power with self-control, moderation and justice. No doubt Cicero was more sensitive than most to resonances between Greek theory and Roman practice. However, the development of the Roman notion of *clementia* ('clemency') tends to support the possibility that the ideology of the 'good governor' played a part in the development of the ideology of the 'good princeps', not least because provincial governorship was the nearest approximation to monarchy that existed under the Republic (Adam 1970; cf.Dorandi 1985).

In fact, Roman governors in the provinces had often replaced kings: they might even, as at Syracuse, use old royal residences (Cic. *In Verr.* 2.4.118). As the first Roman prefect of Egypt, Cornelius Gallus was very conscious that he had succeeded royalty (*ILS* 8995) ; Tacitus observes that prefects of Egypt stood 'in place of kings' (Tac.*Hist.*1.11). Even under the Principate comparisons were made between Roman governors and kings (Tac.*Agr.*15). Amid the chaos of AD 69 the Roman governor of Mauretania, Lucceius Albinus, assumed royal insignia and changed his name to Juba, a name redolent of the royal dynasty his office had replaced (Tac.*Hist.* 2. 58 with Braund 1984, 84). It is therefore no great surprise that the advice given by Menander Rhetor at the end of the third century AD on how to speak in praise of a governor recalls both Cicero and the monarchical theory upon which he had drawn (Russell and Wilson 1981; cf.Juv.*Sat.*8.87ff.). From earliest times provincials and others had commonly regarded Rome and Roman magistrates (including the *princeps*) as being, or being like, kings (Richardson 1979 ; Millar 1984).

Cicero stresses that the good governor (like the good king) must take particular care in choosing and controlling his friends (Cic.*ad Q.fr.*1.1). This was important because the governor took such friends with him as his assistants and advisers, in addition to the few assistants who were furnished by the state (on whom, see Burton 1987, 425; Wiseman 1971, 72-4). Once again private arrangements were thus made to supplement the deficiencies of the state's personnel: the central role of personal patronage in Roman society made such arrangements desirable to all concerned, though provincials might suffer from the depredations of these 'friends' (Braund 1988).

With the advent of the Principate there was both change and continuity. The number of Romans concerned with provincial administration remained minimal, while their approach to administration remained amateurish (Levick and 1985, and with Garnsey and Saller 1982, 15ff. on developments through the first two centuries AD). The emperor now appointed some governors, while the Senate appointed others by lot under usual circumstances. The emperor appointed those governors whose posts required that they command legions and some whose posts did not (as usually in equestrian provinces: see below), while the Senate's appointees usually commanded only a small body of troops (Africa was notably exceptional: Tac.*Hist.*4.48 with Syme 1939, 314). Imperial legates, who were the appointees and agents of the emperor, had no fixed term of office, but a period of three years became commonplace: Cassius Dio makes Maecenas recommend to Augustus a period of three to five years as the ideal term (Dio 52.23 with Syme 1939, 327). The Senate's appointees normally served for one year. Under the Principate most governors through the whole empire were of senatorial rank, but a minority of governors in imperial provinces were of equestrian status - including, most importantly, the prefect of Egypt (Tac.*Ann.*2.59; *Hist.*1.11). Equestrian governors usually held the title of procurator from Claudius onwards, as that title came to replace the title of prefect in most cases: they were appointed by the emperor and usually held office for several years (for an authoritative and lucid exposition, see Burton 1987, 424). The governor's friends still played a large part in administration and could still get out of control (Tac.*Hist.*4.14); Agricola is praised for proper strictness with his friends (Tac.*Agr.*9, quoted below). Ulpian presents the control of such 'assistants' as a specific part of the governor's task (*Digest* 1.18.3).

The division between imperial and senatorial provinces has commonly been exaggerated. Under the Principate, despite this division, the Senate continued to pass decrees and emperors made decisions which applied to all provinces alike (Garnsey and Saller 1982, 16). The emperor could and did issue instructions to governors of senatorial provinces (Levick 1985,

10-11; Burton 1976). And the allocation of a province to the emperor or to the Senate might be changed, as with Achaea in the first century AD and Bithynia in the second, amongst others (Sherwin-White 1966, 526-7 with Stevenson 1949, 103-4). It is worth remembering also that, with the exception of the equestrian prefect of Egypt, those appointed by Augustus to governorships which entailed the command of legions were senior senators (Garnsey and Saller 1982, 19). Moreover, the emperor himself was very much a senator (Millar 1977, 350).

Under the Principate, the collection of taxes was largely taken out of the hands of private tax-farmers. In imperial provinces it was placed under the control of an imperial official, who was, again, called a procurator and was also of equestrian status. The emperor assigned such a procurator to each imperial province to oversee taxation: central to the procurator's task was liaison and co-operation with the cities of his province which bore the brunt of both taxation and the maintenance of order (see Reynolds in this volume; cf.Jones 1974, ch.8 with Burton 1987, 425ff. and Garnsey and Saller 1987). Other procurators were also active in the provinces, dealing in particular with the emperor's many properties there and impinging heavily on those who lived and worked in them (Millar 1977, 180-1; Saller 1983; Garnsey and Saller 1987, 23). In senatorial provinces financial matters were supervised by quaestors, but members of the imperial household were everywhere, in charge of the imperial estates, which were, likewise, everywhere.

Evident in the system is the potential for conflict between such a procurator and the governor of the province in which he functioned. The concerns of the procurator could be narrowly financial, whereas the governor might take a broader view. When Tacitus gives his conception of the 'good governor', as personified by Agricola, he says much that is reminiscent of Cicero's ideal. In accordance with the changes which had taken place under the Principate, Tacitus praises Agricola for his good relations with procurators, where Cicero had dwelt on the governor's relations with tax-farmers:

> Yet Agricola, with his natural good sense, though called to act among civilians, did his work with justice and a light hand. He kept business and relaxation apart. For, when the assize-courts required it, he displayed dignity, concentration and strictness and, still more commonly, clemency. But when business had been completed, he laid aside the mask of power: he was in no way gloomy, arrogant or rapacious. Most unusually, his affability did not weaken his authority, and his strictness did not diminish his popularity. To speak of honesty and restraint in a man of his stature would be an insult to his virtues. He did not seek a good reputation [*fama*]

by parading his virtues or by subterfuge - often a weakness even of good men: he kept well away from rivalry with his colleagues, and well away from conflicts with procurators, for he considered such victories no honour and defeat disgrace. (Tac.*Agr*.9; cf.*Ann*.14.38).

The role of the *publicani* had been reduced largely to the collection of indirect taxes, such as harbour-duties (*portoria*), where they were replaced through the second century AD first by *conductores* and then by still more procurators (Garnsey and Saller 1982, 16 and 1987).

Plutarch says that the future emperor Galba, when Nero's legate in Spain, could do nothing to stop rapacious procurators except to turn a blind eye to the circulation within his province of insulting verses about the emperor (Plut.*Galba* 4). When Nero wanted Galba killed, it was to the procurators that he sent his orders; in the event it was Galba who killed them, together with their families (Suet.*Galba* 9; 12).

Our sources tend to give the impression that the government of the provinces under the Principate was for the most part an improvement upon that of the Republic. Certainly that is the impression that emperors wanted to create: Augustus stresses the energetic beneficence of his regime to provincials (*EJ* 311; cf.Tac.*Ann*.13.50). Indeed, it is not improbable that under the more centralised and more closely controlled circumstances of the Principate, the impression is accurate— after all, an improvement upon the standards of the Republic need be no great advance. Under the Republic governors had used personal connections with provincials to obtain eulogies (and thus an enhancement of their reputations) despite maladministration: Augustus took measures to stop this practice, for it weakened one of the most important extra-legal checks upon the governor (Dio 56.25.6, though see Braund 1988).

However, occasional prosecutions of governors and the complaints (and sometimes uprisings: Tac.*Ann*.3.40; *Hist*.4.14) of provincials indicate that much was still not well. In the second century AD, Juvenal makes it clear that the good conduct of a governor could not be taken for granted (8.87ff., where his remarks seem to have a contemporary relevance): he makes the connection between a governor's misconduct and rebellion in his province (8.112-24). Pliny gives detailed insight into instances of apparent maladministration at much the same time (Talbert 1980 with Brunt 1961 and the remarks of Garnsey and Saller 1982, 17).

The success of the Roman empire depended in great measure upon the good will of the local elites who bore the brunt of local administration.

In addition to Roman maladministration (and in part perhaps in explanation of it), an array of negative Roman attitudes threatened that good-
will. Romans often found it easy to sneer at the various cultures of the
empire: stereotypes abounded—moronic, muscle-bound westerners, wily,
weedy easterners and many more besides (Balsdon 1979). Yet such negative attitudes were in part counterbalanced by Roman interest in and even
respect for at least some of these cultures. Most obviously, despite commonplace contempt for Greeks, Romans admired and were greatly influenced by
Greek culture: Roman ambivalence about Greek philosophy indicates the
confusion which could result from such inconsistency (Brunt 1975). The
prime cause of confusion was that the Greeks, though politically and militarily subordinate to Roman power, exerted so mighty an influence upon
Roman culture—in Horace's words, 'Greece, captured, captured its savage
conqueror' (Horace *Epistles* 2.1.156). Roman imperialism was not only a
matter of wars and diplomacy ; it was also a process of cultural interaction.
And that interaction became increasingly fervent and, indeed, productive as
Rome became the centre of artistic patronage, particularly with the demise
of so many of the old hellenistic court establishments in the Late Republic
(Wiseman 1985a). Moreover, that interaction involved other cultures too,
albeit to a lesser degree: for example, Cicero and his brother seem to have
discussed matters of divination with Diviciacus of the Gallic Aedui, who
was Cicero's guest-friend (*hospes*: Cic.*De Div.* 1.90). It is reasonable to
talk of 'Romanisation' in so far as Roman culture had a profound influence upon certain local cultures, but it should also be remembered that
cultural influence was by no means all one-way, from Rome outwards (on
Romanisation, see Hanson in this volume).

The very term 'Roman' could only develop broader evocations as non-
Romans gained Roman citizenship and thereafter admission to the upper
echelons of the Roman state (Sherwin-White 1973). The great strength of
the Roman state had long been its ability to incorporate others, first in
Italy and then beyond. As early as 215 BC Philip V of Macedon pointed
this out in a letter to Larissa, impressed no doubt by Rome's ability to
sustain the massive losses she had suffered in the early years of the Second
Punic War (*Syll 3.* 543, quoted and discussed by Walbank 1981, 150).
Some members of the older families and the more traditionally-minded of
the Roman elite appreciated the point rather less well than Philip: Cicero
himself had been insulted for being a parvenu (*inquilinus*: Sall.*Cat.*31.7
with Wiseman 1971). Under the Principate, Claudius' admission of Gauls
not simply to the citizenship but to the Senate met considerable hostility:
against such exclusivity Claudius stressed the fact that Roman history had
been a long process of such incorporation and that Rome had become all

the stronger for it. Myths of common Trojan ancestry between Rome and at least some Gauls oiled the wheels of integration and helped to counter folk memories of the Gallic sack of Rome at the beginning of the fourth century BC (*ILS* 212 with Tac.*Ann.*11.23ff. and Braund 1980). It was not long before the first of many emperors of provincial origin came to power in AD 98 in the person of Trajan (albeit, in his case, from an essentially Italian family): by now men of provincial origin and even kings sat in the Senate at Rome. Yet it is hard to see any substantial change in Roman ideology as a result of this continued process of incorporation: Cicero—like his counterparts under the Principate, as far as we can judge—saw himself very much as a defender of Roman traditions, not an agent of their change. It is hard to judge the extent to which Roman traditions actually did change, despite this conservative ideology.

The empire at large had been brought under closer and more centralised control by the emperors (Bowersock 1965), but it remained notably diverse for all that. Latin was the Roman language, but Greek was hardly less important, being the *lingua franca* of the East—'our two tongues' as Claudius described Latin and Greek (Suet.*Claud.*42.1, though note also *Claud.*16.2; cf.Cic.*De Off.*1.1; Hor.*Odes* 3.8.5 etc.). In all parts of the empire, including even Italy, local languages and cultures continued to flourish and gained some recognition under Roman law (Millar 1968). Local traditions survived (cf.Bernhardt 1985). The peculiar administrative structure of Egypt indicates the extent to which the Roman government was willing to accept diversity where local practices worked and did not constitute any sort of threat.

Much of the business of imperial government was conducted in the form of diplomacy, wherein cities sent delegations and letters to governors (as the tenth book of Pliny's letters shows) and ultimately to the emperor with congratulations and requests (Millar 1977, 410-20; Talbert 1980; cf.Price 1984 on the religious aspects of these relationships). These cities retained a definite local identity and a local patriotism within the framework of empire (see Reynolds in this volume). Diplomacy played a very great part not only in the expansion of Roman power and influence, but also in the process of government itself (cf.Magie 1950, 473; Sherwin White 1973, 188). Members of local elites could hope not only to retain their privileges and prestige, but also, should they wish, to advance beyond purely local significance even to become senators or powerful imperial functionaries—possibly even emperors. The Roman empire gave these elites opportunities and in general made their positions more secure within the Roman peace, while it condemned the lower orders to continued subjection, albeit a peaceful one. Taxes were, in theory and to a great extent in practice, the price of peace (Cic.*ad Q.fr*.1.1; Tac.*Hist*.4.74; Dio 52.28.6). It is significant that those who did not pay direct taxes, such as Italians and client kings, were expected to contribute troops (North 1981, 7; Braund 1984, 63-6 and 184).

That revolts against Rome were relatively uncommon is in great part a result of the advantages that local elites enjoyed under Roman rule. It must also be remembered that only the desperate or the foolhardy would lightly rise against the power of Rome, as Agrippa II is said to have pointed out on the eve of the Jewish revolt of AD 66-70 (Jos.*BJ* 2.345ff.). Foreign peoples might actively seek admission to the empire:

> On the whole, emperors wish to preserve the best part of the world —which they hold—through prudence rather than to extend their rule interminably over poverty-stricken, profit-less barbarian peoples, some of whom I have seen at Rome as envoys, offering themselves to be subjects; the emperor did not accept them, for they would be of no use to him. Emperors give kings to countless other peoples, whom they do not require to be under their own rule. In relation to some of their subjects they spend more than they receive, being ashamed to give them up despite the expense. (Appian *Preface* 7; cf.Millar 1982).

In the second century AD, when Appian was writing, the empire was not considered a static thing: the creation of new provinces could be envisaged and continued to be attempted from time to time (Birley 1966 and 1971). The ideology of conquest and expansion remained strong: the emperor still needed to show military prowess—if not in the field, then, like Commodus, in the arena. Prestige is still very much at issue. But Appian indicates a certain caution and a greater (though not entirely overwhelming) concern for the financial consequences of expansion, beyond a desire for booty, than is obvious under the Republic (cf.Strabo 4.p.200 with Levick 1985, 2-3).

The Roman empire was notably long-lived by comparison with most other empires. Military strength was fundamental to that success, but so too was the incorporation of foreigners, which contributed so much to that strength. Military service promoted Romanisation (Vell.Pat.2.110); military camps and colonial settlements of soldiers around the Mediterranean world, from the time of Caesar onwards, contributed not only to the military infrastructure of the empire, but also to the distribution of Roman culture, as had similar colonies long before in the course of the Roman conquest of Italy (Keppie 1984). Roman tolerance and openness to local elites—albeit imperfect and inconsistent—made revolt, under most circumstances, a dangerous nonsense for all but the disadvantaged, who lacked organisation and leaders. The elite might offer some resistance to Roman imperialism at first, but that resistance was usually replaced before long by resignation and co-operation, as local elites saw their only possible future as becoming part of the administration of the Roman empire.

Cities

JOYCE REYNOLDS

Cities were the main centres of life and of local administration in the Roman world. There were very large numbers of them; some 900 are recorded in a survey of the cities of the eastern provinces (Jones 1971). Many areas might be described as a mosaic of cities. They were, strictly speaking, 'peoples' (*populi, demoi*), properly designated by an ethnic rather than a place name (*Carthaginienses* rather than *Carthago*, *Pergamenoi* rather than *Pergamon*). Each occupied and owned a combination of urban centre and rural territory. In principle, these communities were hereditary groups of families (with their dependants). Originally they were very unwilling to admit foreigners into their full membership or to allow them to own any part of their land, though in the Roman imperial period this exclusiveness was distinctly weakened.

Each city was quite formally organised, with civic rights and obligations for its members and a recognised code of laws and institutions through which its affairs were managed, theoretically by the adult male citizens. The urban centre, in which the majority of its members normally lived, was the location of the main meeting-places of the citizens and of their appointed officials: it was the seat of government and judiciary, the major focus of religious and social activity, of manufacture and of markets. In the rural territory were situated further cult places, hamlets and sometimes villages with some subordinate local organisation, as well as isolated farmhouses and, on occasion, points of defence. This rural territory was the source of basic food supplies for all. It was also the source of essential raw materials such as wool, leather, wood, clay for ceramics and, with luck, metals. As far as possible, the necessities of life were produced in the territory and processed in the urban centre. In this way urban centre and rural territory complemented each other and together constituted a unit which was political, social, cultural and economic at the same time. Since that unit—the city— commanded all the resources of its neighbourhood, it offered to a ruling power a convenient medium through which those resources could be controlled. When the ruling power became more sophisticated, it was an equally convenient medium through which loyalty could be organised. The administration of oaths of loyalty to the peoples of the empire through the civic magistrates is an interesting feature of the imperial period (see, for example, *OGIS* 532 at Gangra in Paphlagonia and *ILS* 190 at Aritia in Lusitania).

Our evidence for the study of cities is defective. The literary writers take cities very much for granted. They provide occasional references which tempt generalisation, but such details may be entirely atypical; and they avoid description, still more analysis. The archaeological evidence, from which one might hope for supplementary information, is uneven in quality and distribution over the Roman world. Only a small proportion of the total number of urban sites has been excavated. Moreover, excavations often include only a small part of the total urban area of each city in which they are undertaken. Excavations of residential sectors are notably rare. Still rarer are surveys and excavations in the rural territories: more of these could give the range of information that is necessary if we are to understand a city as a complete whole.

Inscriptions on stone come somewhere between the literary sources and the material remains—discovered as a result of archaeological investigation, but presenting the written word. They record what a city or its citizens considered worthy of preservation; how often they were actually read must remain uncertain (Reynolds, Beard and Roueché 1986, 125, 142-3). Since excavators of urban sites have, on the whole, paid most attention to their public places and to their cemeteries, we should be rather well off for public inscriptions and funeraries. It must be remembered, however, that the habit of inscribing on stone was more common in some cities than in others, not least because good stone, suitable for the cutting of letters, was not readily available to every city. Moreover, the chances which have preserved what was inscribed on one site (and brought it to light) did not obtain on many others. And, as the example of Pompeii shows, there might be many notices painted rather than cut on the walls of an ancient city, and many ephemeral graffiti that were scratched on them by casual writers. Where special conditions have preserved these in any numbers, as at Pompeii, their discovery throws a world of new light both on public and on private life (Etienne, 1974); but it is very unusual for that to be the case. In the West especially, inscriptions, including the very important city constitutions, were often cut on bronze tablets, which were liable to be melted down for re-use when their texts ceased to be relevant. And more than we can possibly know may well have been cut on wood, which decays quickly under normal conditions.

There are, then, problems of evidence. But a quite vivid picture can be drawn nevertheless, even if many points remain obscure.

The Romans who reached out from Italy into overseas empire from the third century BC onwards were themselves in origin a city community. They are notorious for their retention of thought-patterns appropriate to such a city, despite the ever-increasing irrelevance of that civic ideology to their new imperial circumstances. The Romans had also gained experience of many other city communities in Italy. Indeed, they had developed means of controlling the resources of these cities, as required, without imposing direct rule. Moreover, in the Greek and Carthaginian worlds into which the Romans expanded, they found many well-established cities: some were the descendants of sovereign city-states of the fifth and fourth centuries BC, others had been founded subsequently on the same pattern. Most had had to learn to live in the shadow of greater powers, usually one of the famous Hellenistic kingdoms— Macedon, Pergamon, Syria, Egypt or, in a smaller way, Syracuse. The favour of kings was necessary for their survival. And royal intervention could very severely limit the free activity of their institutions. The relationships between these cities and kings were, then, broadly analogous to those between the Italian cities and Rome. For that reason, despite difficulties in particular cases, cities could easily find and be allowed a position and role as Rome created a system of empire.

The Romans regulated their relations with each city according to the circumstances in which those relations began—whether in formal agreement by treaty, agreement for cooperation on a less formal basis, or, conversely, in opposition and defeat. Changes could be introduced thereafter as occasion suggested, as, for instance, after a notable display of loyalty. So the city of Aphrodisias in Caria (S.W. Turkey) received freedom, immunity from taxation and a formal treaty in 39 BC, after its resistance to the invasion of Asia Minor by Parthians led by Labienus (Reynolds 1982a, document 8). But intransigence towards Rome, actual or imagined, could bring about a change for the worse, as in the well-known case of Rhodes after 167 BC (Polybius, 30.5.11-16). A consequence of the haphazard and piecemeal creation and development of Roman relations with the many cities of her empire was complex variation—some cities had very privileged treaties of alliance with Rome and/or the name of freedom, together with freedom from taxation and other levies, while others (the majority) had not. All cities, however, were expected to carry on reasonably effective local government through their city institutions. In particular, they were expected to maintain local order and to meet Rome's demands for tax. More broadly, they should exhibit loyalty to her and support her interests, together with those of her individual citizens.

For the cities, this arrangement had the advantage of a continued life in some accordance with their own traditions. For the Romans, it provided local order without much expense or trouble and a ready-made organisation through which levies could be raised. And the Romans therefore sought to expand the city system in areas of their eastern empire where, as in Bithynia-Pontus, it was weak. Moreover, they encouraged the development of cities on a very considerable scale when they expanded into areas of the West where cities had barely existed, if at all, before they came.

It was probably inevitable that Romans would become involved, as they did from quite early on, in interventions in individual cities. Their aim was to reinforce loyalty and, as they saw it, no doubt, to improve standards of administration or to save communities which appeared to be faltering. Since our evidence seldom allows us to draw distinctions between cities and their governing elites, Roman interventions can also be seen as help for the loyal governing class—or loyal factions within the governing class—and that usually meant the rich.

The size of the cities was very variable. In the fifth century BC Hippodamus of Miletus, town-planner, argued for a population of 10,000 adult male citizens. In the fourth the philosopher Plato proposed around 5,000 for an ideal city, and Aristotle thought that too many (Aristotle, *Politics* 2.5.2, 5.3.2 and 3). Small size was, surely, the norm, for the difficulty of feeding large agglomerations of people was a potent limiting factor. On the other hand, in the second century AD the doctor Galen (5.49 Kuhn) posited some 40,000 adult male citizens, with an allowance of a further 80,000 persons for wives and slaves, at Pergamon in western Asia Minor. However, this was a city with a large territory, which was probably much more fertile than the land of mainland Greece to which Plato and Aristotle were accustomed. With further allowances (for children, resident aliens and free non-citizen dependants), it has been thought that the total population of Pergamon in Galen's time might have been around 200,000 (Broughton 1938, p.812). Near the sea, or on a navigable river, a city had the opportunity to import supplementary food supplies, especially after Rome had created a kind of unity in the Mediterranean world and substantially cleared the seas of pirates. By contrast, in the interiors of the provinces the transportation of supplementary supplies was very difficult. For that very reason, few cities can have been as large as Pergamon, very few indeed were larger. It is conjectured that the population of imperial Rome was around 1,000,000, but Rome was quite exceptional and food for its inhabitants was provided by a quite exceptional effort on the part of the emperors. A recent survey of the evidence which has been used to estimate city sizes (not all of it satisfactory) suggests that some cities were very small indeed - Corfinium in Italy less than 3,000, Fabrateria in Italy less than 2,000 (Duncan Jones 1982, ch.6). Naturally the geographical areas covered by the city territories were variable in size too. On occasion they might even be extended by the acquisition of land elsewhere—so the island-city of Cos possessed lands on Cyprus (Sherwin White, 1975). No less variable were the range and quality of the civic amenities provided.

When a new city was created in the Roman empire (from scratch or by elevation of an existing village), we may suppose that some thought was given to its economic viability, with a view to the maintenance of administration and amenities at a reasonable level. That concern can be glimpsed in a letter of the emperor Constantine on the elevation to city status of the Phrygian village of Orcistus (*MAMA* 5.30, cf. Chastagnol 1981): it had, he wrote, a large population, good public buildings, a site at an important road centre and a plentiful supply of water, which was being used to power mills. The principle is good, but the assessment is quite superficial - it may even be suspected that the emperor has simply taken over the words in which the Orcistans themselves had urged their case for the promotion. Among older cities—and newer ones too from time to time—changing circumstances (a silted harbour perhaps, or an exhausted quarry) produced decline for some, while others prospered beyond what might have been expected (for examples of both, see Syme 1981).

Archaeologists, who have tended to excavate what promised to be rich sites (especially in the Mediterranean area), have created some expectation that all cities had grandiose public monuments. It is indeed true that there was competition in display among cities in the Roman period (very notable and well-authenticated in Asia Minor). At the same time there was also a competition for glory among the leading citizens which often led them to make lavish gifts of public buildings and other donations to their cities. Such attitudes generated many grand civic centres. But these should not lead us to forget the cities that were not grand. Early in the second century AD the rhetor and local politician Dio Chrysostom of Prusa in Bithynia described a city on the Greek island of Euboea (perhaps Carystus) in which the *agora*, namely the central market-place and meeting-place, was used as a grazing ground for cattle, while the *palaestra*, the exercise-ground, had been ploughed up (*Or.* 7). A little later the travel-writer Pausanias noted that the Phocian city of Panopeus in mainland Greece lacked offices for magistrates, gymnasium, theatre, agora, public fountain and houses that deserved a better name than hovels (10.4.1). These two cities may have been exceptionally bad (it is commonly held that Greece was economically depressed in the Roman imperial period), but we should not lightly assume that there were no others like them. And there were probably many whose public places were quite simple compared with those of Pergamon, for instance, or Ephesus. Thus both Dio of Prusa and the younger Pliny indicate that in their time there were a number of poor, and some ruined, buildings in the centre of Prusa (*Or.* 40, 47; Plin.*Epp.* 10.2).

The civic centres, however, normally aimed to provide open spaces and architecture of some pretensions, with porticoes and colonnades of marble or, failing that, imitation marble created by plastering and painting stone or brick. The residential areas, to judge from our limited evidence, would present, by contrast, very simple facades of plastered brick, often mud-brick, fronting narrow streets, even when the accommodation behind the facades was gracious and elegant, with ornamental gardens in the court-yards. And these residences were not necessarily separated from areas of entertainment, production and sales. Public baths might be sited within them and, as at Pompeii, for instance, shops, workshops, bars etc. were sometimes incorporated into the street frontages of houses. It is not clear whether blocks of flats like those built in Rome and at Ostia were com-monplace (Meiggs 1973, ch.12). Residential areas seem often to have been crowded, but, for all that, it is likely that in country towns they contained cultivated open spaces—at Pompeii, for example, a vineyard is attested in a residential area (Jashemski 1979)

Most of the well-to-do probably owned their own houses, but some seem to have rented: 'gentlemen's' apartments to let were advertised at Pompeii (*CIL* 4.1136). The poor normally rented (Dio Chrys. *Or.*7.105) and sometimes lived in the small workshops (*tabernae* or *ergasteria*) in which they also made their living (Meiggs 1973, ch.13). Particular districts or streets sometimes became associated with particular trades (MacMullen

1974, 132f.). In addition, booths were set up as further points of sale in public places—and not only in markets at that. Nor were even booths necessary, for goods could be simply spread out for display on the ground. Some men established particular locations for booths or simple displays: they scratched or painted notices beside them to show that this was their particular pitch (Etienne 1974 gives examples from Pompeii). There were also hawkers who carried their goods around the streets and squares or into the public baths and theatres.

For the appearance of the countryside there is not much evidence. In some sophisticated areas of Italy, such as Campania, a degree of suburbanisation is suggested. Most territories were probably really rural, although it may well be that there was a natural tendency to develop market-gardens in the immediate neighbourhood of the towns, since associations of market-gardeners sometimes appear alongside those of urban craftsmen (e.g. at Carian Aphrodisias, unpublished). In many territories there will no doubt have been some large villas, perhaps with 'holiday' accommodation for owners whose main residence was in the town along with basic accommodation for farm-workers (Cotton 1979, 1985). But what the housing of peasants was like is not clear. Dio draws a pretty picture of the simple but adequate huts of his Euboean huntsmen (*Or.* 7.64f.), with vines outside the doors (7.46). One of these men is credited with a son-in-law described as a rich man and living in a village (7.68), but little is said of his house in the village ; since it has no garden, its owner must get his fruit and green vegetables from his father-in-law to whom, on the other hand, he has 'lent' wheat for seed—so he was a farmer. In so far as any of this is realistic, it is reasonable to suppose that 'rich' is a very relative term here and that the rich village house was not so very grand. A village might have some 'public' monuments of its own (a temple or shrine at least, and a square to provide a small market place). It could, like Orcistus (above), develop a good deal more in lucky circumstances, but more villages in city territories are likely to have been simple than lucky. We are unable to distinguish the accommodation of peasant citizens of any city from that of dependent peoples of that city, living and working in the same civic territory (where such peoples might constitute the bulk of the labour-force, as commonly in Asia Minor).

An important feature of Rome's encouragement of the city system was her establishment of new cities (urban centres with territories in which land allotments were made) for colonists who were usually time-expired soldiers, although some selected natives might be joined with them. In the Republican and early imperial periods the soldier-colonists were commonly men from Italy. But increasingly, as army recruitment came to draw on the manpower of the provinces, they became men of much more varied origin. They constituted both unofficial garrisons (*propugnacula imperii*, Cic.*de leg.agr.*2.73) and 'images of the people of Rome' (*effigies...populi Romani*, Aulus Gellius 16.13), models of the Roman way of life which all locals might imitate.

Less formal models were available in some districts, namely Italians present in local communities—merchants for instance who might take up temporary residence while in pursuit of their business concerns. They sometimes stayed for long periods. There were also refugees from Rome, seeking permanent homes in exile, particularly in troubled times such as the first century BC. All these brought not only their private life-styles, but also patterns of organisation. Groups of them tended to form associations (*conventus*) for cult and other social activities, which were themselves organised in ways reminiscent of the Italian city governments. Such men tended to dominate the cities in which they lived, to the point that civic action might be recorded as the joint decision of the city and themselves (cf.*IGRR* 4.248, 903, 919). And their dominance might be very bitterly resented, as is suggested by the wholesale massacre of such 'immigrants' at the instigation of King Mithridates of Pontus, when he invaded Roman Asia in 88 BC (Appian, *Mithridatica* 23). This event must be some index of their importance. Occasionally we can see the cultural effects of their presence—thus perhaps in the introduction of South Italian designs (many of the Roman businessmen came from Campania) to building-works in the cities of North Africa (Ward Perkins 1970, 15-18). Still more indicative is the developing use of Latin in western communities. Cultural influence is more elusive in the East. There the immigrants sometimes married into the local citizen families and took on Greek identities, without, however, necessarily abandoning their Italian identities, which could prove useful for certain purposes (Reynolds 1982b).

In the West locals certainly imitated the models available to them, often, it seems, on their own initiative, but sometimes, no doubt, as the advantages to Rome came to be recognised, after prompting from Roman officials. It is well known that C.Julius Agricola led the British elite to build Roman-style public works in the towns of Britain and adopt Roman culture (Tacitus, *Agricola* 21). Agricola was not alone in this. There are a number of inscriptions which show other governors making similar moves throughout the empire. A good instance is the action of a governor of Africa at Lepcis Magna during the reign of Tiberius. The governor restored to that city a sum of money temporarily lost from its income (we can only guess, unsatisfactorily, at what lies behind this) and saw to it that the money was used to pave the city's streets (*IRT* 330- 31). Another case in point is that of a governor of Sardinia under Domitian. He organised the use of civic funds, swollen by private donations (which he had, no doubt, stimulated), to pave a public square and streets and to construct and cover drains at Carales (*ILS* 5350). In the West (but not in the East) the result was often very marked Romanisation—thus the elder Pliny could describe southern France (Provence) as more like Italy than a province (*NH* 3.4.32). Where cultural assimilation was promisingly advanced, an encouragement to take it further was the grant of improved civic status in the Roman hierarchy. Eventually this policy produced a kind of ladder of seniority for cities, in which the rungs were, from bottom to top:

(1) native ('peregrine') city.
(2) municipality with minor Latin rights—where the town was given a charter for a Latin-type constitution, all citizens had the privileges associated with Latium, the area of Italy with which Rome was most closely linked by race and language: ex-magistrates, together with some members of their families, received Roman citizenship.
(3) municipality with major Latin rights—as for (2), except that all members of the municipal council received Roman citizenship.
(4) municipality of Roman citizens—where not only did the community have a Latin-type constitution, but all its citizens also had Roman citizenship.
(5) Roman citizen colony—where, if the city was not itself a settlement of citizen-colonists, it was deemed to be such, and was given charter, privileges and prestige accordingly.
(6) Roman citizen colony with Italian rights—where the colony's land was deemed to be the land of Italy and so exempt from direct Roman taxation: this of course was a comparatively rare grant (Abbott and Johnson 1926).

The scheme was sufficiently flexible to accommodate not only communities which might have formed a recognisable city in any part of the Roman world, but also tribal groups (or segments of tribes) as, notably, in native Spain, Gaul, Germany and Britain. Tribal organisations, located in a tribal capital, evolved into something indistinguishable in their known activities and monuments from cities, even when the sense of tribal identity survived strongly, as is demonstrated by the evolution of such a name as Paris from *Lutetia Parisiorum*.

The Greek cities of the eastern half of the Roman empire were not inter-ested in this degree of assimilation to Roman culture. Particular elements in it they might accept, even welcome,— baths, for instance, amphitheatres and gladiatorial games. But they had a strong civic tradition of their own and a language and literature in which they took pride and which they were not disposed to abandon for what the Romans had to offer. A certain number of Roman colonies were settled in the eastern provinces. Alexan-dria Troas in western Asia Minor, Sinope in Bithynia-Pontus, Antiocheia in Galatia and Berytus in Syria are examples (for the history of one group of colonies, see Levick 1967 with Bowie 1970). But these colonies were not treated as models to be closely imitated. And they might take on quite a lot of colour from their native neighbours, as at Cremna in Lycia (Robert, 1973).

The western ladder of civic seniority had no place in the Greek East. There, an aspiring village aimed to be promoted to the status of a Greek city. And an existing Greek city sought enhanced prestige in other ways, as in the official grant of freedom to use its own laws, and in immunity from taxation (but that was rarely given, at any rate in the imperial period). Also highly valued were statuses associated with the position of provincial cap-ital (the main centre of provincial government) and of assize-town (where the governor or his deputy came regularly to hold judicial sessions), or of metropolis (where the common council of representatives of the cities of a province, or of a section of a province, met), or of *neokoros* (where there was a temple at which the rituals of imperial cult were performed in the name of a whole province or of a section of one). It should be observed, however, that there were disadvantages connected with some of these 'honours'. Thus the presence of a governor and his staff might entail expenditure on their entertainment, as well as exposure to their attention, with the possibility of more intervention in civic affairs than might otherwise have occurred. Nevertheless such disadvantages were outweighed by the advantages to be gained. Where the governors held their courts, as Dio of Prusa pointed out (*Or.* 35.15), there was an influx of people bringing profits to those who catered for their board and lodging. And such visitors might well spend money on other things too, in the manner of tourists. Moreover the citizens of an assize-town could normally expect to have their own cases heard in their own city and so to avoid the expense and inconvenience of going else-where to a court. Among the more vivid pieces of evidence showing that the benefits were generally appreciated is an inscribed letter in which An-toninus Pius responded to a petition from the Cyrenaican city of Berenice which hoped to become an assize-town. Having stated that the governor did not have time for the additional travelling, the emperor observed that it would not be fair to reduce the advantages of the existing assize-towns of the province, at least without their agreement (*SEG* 28 1566, lines 69-77).

Rivalry between cities for genuine advantages seems easily to have generated unreasonable emotions in both East and West alike. In the East, for example, Dio of Prusa tells of the passions aroused by competition between Nicomedeia and Nicaea (*Or.* 38). An inscription reveals the complaint sent to Antoninus Pius by the Ephesians because Smyrna had failed to address them with all their proper titles (*Syll 3.* 849, lines 8-15). In the West, civic rivalry led to a bloodstained riot between Pompeians and Nucerians in the amphitheatre of Pompeii in AD 59 (Tacitus, *Ann.* 14.17 ; the affair is illustrated in a sketch at Pompeii: see Etienne 1974, 429). And it was in the context of civic rivalry that the people of Oea in North Africa decided to invite Garamantians from outside the Roman frontier to assist them in raiding the territory of their neighbours, the people of Lepcis Magna, in AD 68-9 (Tacitus, *Hist.* 4.50). Undoubtedly civic patriotism could still be, in many places in the Roman empire, a very strong force and that force was not always usefully directed.

The standard institutions of civic government throughout the empire were annual magistracies and city councils. Magistrates were elected by an assembly of adult male citizens, which could also be called upon (by the magistrates qualified to preside over it) to vote on other matters when these had been previously discussed by the city council. The names and numbers of magistrates and councils differed from city to city, as also did the precise distribution of functions and responsibilities among them. The relationship of these institutions to one another could also vary markedly to produce a range of constitutional colourings from full-scale democracy to closed oligarchy, though Roman sympathies were largely with the latter.

It so happens that a number of inscriptions have survived in Italy and Spain (mostly of the first century BC and the first century AD) which preserve quite extensive sections of Roman legal documents concerned with city government (among older documents note especially *ILS* 6085-9). These documents show us what the Romans themselves thought desirable and might impose. Characteristic features were:

(1) qualifications for magisterial offices based on:

wealth (amounts varying from city to city),

age (30 years seems to have been a common lower limit under the Republic, but it is known to have been reduced to 22 in Bithynia-Pontus by a decision of Augustus (Pliny, *Epp.* 10.79) which may well have been of more general application—variation from city to city is probable),

status (normally free-born citizen origin) and character (unblemished by criminal conviction or by participation in such occupations as were thought disgracing).

(2) life-membership for members of city councils, who were selected, basically from ex-magistrates, by senior magistrates appointed to go through the lists every fourth year.

(3) careful control of the citizen-assemblies by the presiding magistrates and perhaps restricted consultation of them.

These features tended to produce oligarchies of the wealthier and older citizens. A small concession to democracy was the use of elections, but in practice the authority of the unelected city councils came to dominate all public affairs, including elections. Long-term city councillors were the advisors (and, in a sense, supervisors) of short-term magistrates.

In the West many city constitutions were imposed in the charters associated with the creation of new cities and awards of new status to old ones. In the East new cities were also 'given' their constitutions and although these incorporated Greek city practice (except in the small number of colonies), they will still have shown the Roman preference for oligarchy. It is also clear that after conquest the Romans sometimes revised old city constitutions in the conquered area, again, in the oligarchic direction, as can be seen in Achaea in 146 BC (*RDGE* 43, lines 9-10). By such procedures and, no doubt, by exerting pressure, they seem to have secured oligarchy virtually throughout the cities of their empire by the end of the Republic. The basis of these oligarchies was life-membership of the city councils for men chosen, not elected, from among the wealthy or comparatively so.

Yet some features of a different tradition seem to have survived. Some eastern city councils remained large (450 members at Ephesus apparently, *I.Eph.* Ia no. 27, lines 222f.). By contrast, in the West, a membership of 100 is commonly said to be the norm and it was sometimes certainly smaller (63 at Irni in Spain, Gonzalez 1986, ch. 31). Large councils, by reason of their size, might find it impossible to maintain their numbers through recruitment of ex-magistrates alone—or, indeed, through recruitment from the classes from which magistrates were traditionally drawn. So we hear of gradings within councils according to social status and wealth (cf. *Digest* 50.7.5.5. (Hadrian)) and of the introduction of members who did not belong to the old elite families (see below). But, whether large or small, councils came to be treated as sources from which magistrates might be drawn rather than as associations of ex-magistrates. They seem increasingly to have decided among themselves who should hold office. At Knossos, for example, in the late second–early third centuries AD it was openly stated that public office had been conferred on a man 'by decree of the decurions' (Chaniotis 1985).

There is also perhaps more evidence for continued activity by citizen assemblies in the East than we have for the West. Of course, it is hard, for any part of the Roman world, to be sure when civic action attributed to 'the people' resulted from a formal vote taken in a properly constituted citizen assembly, and when it followed from an expression of feeling, by cheers or chanting of the slogans called acclamations (Roueché, 1984) —or, conversely, by hisses and boos—in an informal or semi-formal gathering in the agora, forum, theatre or amphitheatre. There may, then, have been more official assemblies than we know in the West, but for the East we have literary references and even some description of them. Plutarch's advice to young city politicians refers to the problems of controlling the people in the assemblies which they must face (*Mor.* 796c-f, 814a, 815a). Dio of Prusa describes one meeting in Euboea which was far from decorous (*Or.* 7.24-63). And he himself spoke before other assemblies—notably one at Prusa where he reminds the citizens that they had only just recovered the right to meet, a right which the governor had suspended because of their disorderly behaviour (*Or.* 48).

But it is as well to remember that even where democratic assemblies had ceased to meet, people might still express their wishes with clarity and force, though not always with success. A few examples of differing character will serve to illustrate the point. Apuleius implied that the pressure of the crowd at Oea extracted from his wife excessive gifts of *sportulae* (literally, baskets of food) at her son's wedding and that he avoided a similar occurrence at his own wedding by celebrating it out of town (*Apol.* 88). The emperor Antoninus Pius rebuked the people of Ephesus for the coolness with which they had received a rich citizen's gift of an odeon when they wanted shows, public entertainments and distributions of food and money (*Syll 3.* 850). Dio Chrysostom reproached the people of Prusa, his own city, for an attack made upon him by a hungry crowd which held him responsible for a famine—'raging at fellow-citizens...refusing to discuss the matter at all with them, and, instead, stoning them and setting fire to their houses in an attempt to burn them to death along with their children and their wives' (*Or.* 46.11). The views of the people might be very well-known and some of the generosity which civic benefactors proclaim in their inscriptions was evidently less than voluntary.

It is, and was, very easy to undervalue what city governments did. Our picture is liable to be clouded by attitudes like that of Horace, who voices contempt for the pretensions of a civic magistrate (*Sat.*1.5.34-6). Similarly, Juvenal indicates that to many the local magistrate, for whose characteristic function he chooses adjudication on weights and measures, was pretty small beer (*Sat.*10.100-2): the buying public might have taken a more favourable view of an activity so much to its advantage. The point underlines the well-known problem of evidence which comes from the upper class and ignores the views of the rest. Then again, prolonged reading of civic inscriptions can create the impression that the citizens' time, thought and money were substantially consumed in the boring award of fulsome and repetitive honours to public benefactors— for the surviving epigraphic evidence is slanted to give undue limelight to one category of text. Plutarch attempts a more balanced evaluation (*Mor.* 805a ff.). It was true, he said, that in his time (the later first and early second centuries AD) the affairs of the cities no longer included leadership in wars, negotiation of alliances or the overthrow of tyrannies; nor would city politicians be wise to forget the existence of a ruling power. But, even so, serious issues did come up for decision by the cities, for there was serious business to do ; the Romans were not so keen to interfere—too often the Greeks appealed to them and brought them in when there was no need to do so (*Mor.* 815a). We can, to some extent, check these points against other evidence, which tends to support Plutarch's claims.

It is not, perhaps, surprising that in the Republican period cities might still need to decide matters of war and peace and to provide the leadership for their own armies if they decided to fight. Cities did just that over a wide area of Asia Minor and Greece when Mithridates of Pontus rose against Rome (cf.Bernhardt 1985). We have, for example, the decrees of the city of Plarasa with Aphrodisias passed in 88 BC, when the armies of Mithridates were defeating the Romans who attempted to check them:

> Agreed by the Council and People...proposal moved by...the
> Secretary to the People and...the General for the Territory:
> ...that they should muster an army and give help in force
> to...the Roman praetor [who was besieged nearby] and, with

> their resident aliens and slaves, should march out under a
> leader chosen by the assembly...also agreed that they should
> despatch ambassadors to inform the praetor of this...and that
> the whole people, together with our wives and children, is
> ready to risk all for...the Roman cause, preferring death to life
> without the rule of the Romans. (Reynolds 1982a, document
> 2).

However, it is easy to forget that comparable crises arose even after the
establishment of the Roman peace, which was never absolute. During Roman civil wars some cities might be far enough from the main theatres of
conflict to evade choice of sides until the outcome was known. Others were
so firmly within the area held by one side or the other that they could
exercise no real choice. But in each Roman civil war some cities had to
choose sides and, if a city backed a loser, the result could be disaster. Such
a disastrous choice was made by Byzantium when it decided to support
Pescennius Niger against Septimius Severus in AD 194 (Cassius Dio 75.10-
14). Roman civil wars were comparatively rare between the end of the
Republic and the middle of the third century AD. But even in less trau-
matic times there were 'bandits' to contend with (raids by combinations
of refugees—runaway slaves, the destitute free and condemned criminals:
Shaw 1984). On occasion, there was even attack from untamed elements
within the empire, especially in remote mountainous and forested districts.
And there were also some invaders from beyond the frontiers, who broke
into areas where there were no protective Roman armies. Thus, in the reign
of Augustus, Cyrene was the target of persistent attacks by nomads on the
fringe of the empire. Against these attacks the city decided to organise her
own defence, on the initiative of a particularly vigorous citizen, who was
himself given the command (for the honours paid to that citizen, see *OGIS*
767). In the reign of Marcus Aurelius when a number of cities in Greece
found themselves on the route of the invading tribe of the Costoboci, Elatea
at least decided to fight, again on the initiative of a particularly vigorous
citizen (Pausanias 10.34.5). Under Commodus, when the cities of Lycia
(and, apparently, Bubon in particular) were harassed by large-scale banditry, Bubon received, and inscribed, a letter from the emperor praising the
zeal and courage with which her citizens had resisted and killed a number
of the enemy, capturing many others alive (Schindler 1972, no. 2). These
cases were certainly not the only ones.

Critical issues which fell short of such a need for self-defence could also
arise, as, for instance, when the Spanish city of Sabora decided to move its
site from the hill-top to the plain below to improve its prospects of prosper-
ity, and applied to the emperor Vespasian for permission (*ILS* 6092). Nor

were relations with neighbours and other cities always purely ceremonial. We do not in fact really know how much was involved when cities celebrated the establishment of what they described as *homonoia* (concord) with other cities (in Asia Minor they often issued memorial coinage). We do know that cities sometimes sharply disagreed with one another, notably about the boundaries of their civic territories: they had then to defend their cases before governors, emperors or arbitrators. Among many known examples is the disagreement between the Delphians and their neighbours which was settled after arbitration by a legate of Hadrian, who had very precise accounts of the agreed boundaries inscribed (*Syll 3*. 827).

Cities also conducted relations with the provincial organisations (which were known as *concilia* in the West, *koina* in the East) to which they sent representatives. These organisations performed cult acts in honour of the emperors. They also discussed matters of common interest, including the merits of governors, who might receive their praises or be prosecuted for extortion. A city needed effective representatives on these bodies. Vital aspects of its relations with Rome were involved. Moreover some collective decisions might affect its everyday management of affairs, as with the decision of the *koinon* of Asia in 9 BC to reform the calendar in use in Asia (the stimulus being the desire to make Augustus' birthday the first day of the year). Copies of that decree were distributed to all member cities; a number of them are known to have had it inscribed and displayed publicly, while all presumably adopted it (*EJ* 98). Not all *koinon* decrees were so acceptable— when the *koinon* of Asia issued what sounds to us like an admirable call to its members to help cities which were victims of earthquake in the reign of Gordian III, the Aphrodisians took it as an instruction which threatened their legal freedom of action; they protested indignantly (Reynolds 1982a, document 21). Foolish though this may seem, it illustrates the sense, which was probably deeply engrained in the cities, that the vital business of preserving their privileges required eternal vigilance against all comers, up to and including the emperor. Gordian's response is worth noting as an expression of an official policy which was not consistently practised:

> The decree of the Council of Asia associating you with those who are assisting the victims of the disaster was not an order, for orders cannot be issued to free men, but a useful proposal which treated you as men of humanity, such indeed as you show among yourselves when you assist those in need to restore a house.

One tactic in the continuous campaign to maintain and, if possible, increase civic privileges was the appointment by the cities of patrons living elsewhere who would help to guard their interests—eminent men in the province and at Rome. The importance of the choice of patrons is clear from the regulations laid down for it in the civic charters and the very formal agreements which were made between cities and their patrons (*ILS* 6093-116, for example). To mobilise the aid of patrons in times of need, ambassadors would have to go to them to present the city's case. An inscription of the reign of Antoninus Pius from Tergeste expresses that city's gratitude to a citizen who had become a Roman senator and had successfully used his opportunities as such to further the city's interests with the emperor. In particular, he had secured a change in the status of the dependent population of the territory so that appropriate men of wealth became eligible for membership of the city council (*ILS* 6680).

Nor should we belittle the routine of city government. On this we can draw profitably upon the very recently discovered and published *Lex Irni-tana* from Spain (Gonzalez 1986) where, among the substantial surviving portions of a civic charter for a Latin municipality with minor rights, two sections list the functions of particular magistracies. Aediles at Irni, we learn, had the right and power to administer the corn supply, the sacred buildings, the sacred and holy places, the town, the roads, the districts, the drains, the baths, the market, the inspection of weights and measures, the watch (when occasion arose for it), anything else assigned to them by the city council, and certain minor jurisdictional matters—for all of which purposes they were allotted a small staff of civically-owned slaves. Quaestors at Irni had the right and power to collect, spend, keep, administer and look after the common funds of the city at the discretion of the chief magistrates, the *duoviri*.

It would have been good to have also a list of the functions of the *duoviri*, but that so far has not come to light. Yet we do know some of their usual duties, such as organising and presiding at meetings of the city council, meetings of the assembly of citizens and sessions of the local courts. And sometimes inscriptions show aspects of other duties—as, for instance, when we see them inspecting newly-erected monuments and superintending or carrying out various religious rituals. All this amounts to a great deal of useful activity, some of it entailing significant responsibility. There is much about which we could wish to know more, however, notably the local courts of justice. Plutarch still regards these courts as arenas in which local politicians could help their friends and make their names (*Mor.* 805a), although in most cities the more important cases went to a Roman court.

In the Irni list of the functions of aediles, the first item is the care of the corn supply. Since one bad harvest might reduce the whole citizen body to near starvation, a city's survival might depend on a prudent control of the basic food supply and on its ability to take emergency action in a crisis. This could not be left to chance. In some cities special officers were appointed with the sole function of overseeing the corn supply. In many cities such officers were appointed when shortage threatened. We have already seen in the case of Prusa what strong feelings could be aroused by shortage: there are numerous testimonies to the efforts of the appointed officials, and to their generous expenditures from their own purses ; for example,

> having been controller of the market at a time of most serious famine, he provided corn at a fair price at his own expense. (Reynolds 1982a, document 30).

After the food, on the list, come the sacred buildings and places, which we may elaborate as covering in essence temples, shrines, altars, sacred enclosures, with theatres, amphitheatres and the like probably included, since the public entertainment presented in them continued to have a close association with cult rituals (as with the theatrical performances in the Theatre of Dionysus in classical Athens). The civic cults brought together all or most citizens (including women and children and often dependants) in performance of acts designed to secure good relations with the ruling powers of the universe and with the ruling powers on earth (Rome, the Emperors, the Roman People, the Roman Senate, cf. Price 1984). They expressed a sense of community in relation to powers external to the city. For the immediate practical purpose of propitiating these powers, they drew upon the city's own traditions, incorporated in literature, music and dance, for instance, so that the ritual occasions might also have a strong cultural significance. What was thought likely to please divinities might well be pleasurable to those who participated in the ritual—holidays, with public feasting and public entertainment (a very important part of the city's life). It is worth remembering that whatever else Pausanias found lacking at Panopeus (above) he did not say that there were no sacred places - it is not and was not possible to envisage an ancient city without them.

Aediles at Irni had also to take care of more mundane features of the physical township—streets, drains, secular public buildings. What the last heading would cover will certainly have varied from city to city. Care of streets might include care of roads in the territory (occasionally milestones record civic activity on these). There might also be provision and mainte- nance of a water supply—aqueduct, cisterns, fountains, water basins with the possibility of a piped supply to private houses (on payment, though we know that payment was often evaded). There might be market-buildings.

There might be city walls. There would be open places for public meetings and commonly some buildings for public affairs, the meeting places of the city council and the courts of law, offices for magistrates and priests, treasury, archive, including an archive for deposit of private documents such as wills and contracts. One such archive-building has been excavated at Cyrene - the documents had been burnt in a destroying fire but the magisterial seals affixed to each on deposit had often survived (Maddoli 1963). There might also be buildings providing amenities for citizens—public baths (for which water, fuel for heating, staff for servicing, and oil for rubbing down must be provided), public gymnasia (again with provision of oil and servicing staff), porticoes, with the shops and offices often built so as to open into them, and some items like monumental arches that were essentially decorative. These made up the physical setting of the citizens' lives, which were spent to a great extent out-of-doors, in the open air, as still happens in a Mediterranean climate: some were essential to them, others gave them the sense of being civilised, urbane, humane—and as good as the next city, if not better.

Rather low on the list of aediles' duties, as it might seem to us, comes 'the watch', perhaps no more than a fire-fighting company, but possibly undertaking some police duties. Arrangements for fire-fighting were everywhere quite rudimentary. In western cities we sometimes hear that craftsmen's clubs (often carpenters) might be expected to act as firemen, when needed, but in the East this system does not seem to have developed. When an unchecked fire damaged Nicomedeia in Bithynia, Pliny organised public provision of useful equipment and proposed the creation of a fire-fighting force on the western analogy. But Trajan forbade it for fear that such a body might become a force for political unrest ; he urged instead more provision of equipment and self-help by property-owners (Pliny, *Epp.*10.33-34).

Policing was similarly rudimentary. Small contingents of Roman soldiers might provide some control in some places, but by and large it fell to the cities to do what they saw fit, which was comparatively little. In some areas, especially in Asia Minor, there are records of officials (often called eirenarchs or paraphylakes) patrolling the territories at the head of armed bands. These forces were commonly recruited from the young men in their later teens who were undergoing gymnastic and paramilitary training provided by the cities (*iuvenes* in the West, ephebes and *neoi* in the East). The intention seems to have been routine control of bandits (above). There are occasional indications that these 'police forces' might have been more trouble than they were worth. Thus the city council of Hierapolis has recorded a decision that, when their duties necessitated an overnight stay in a village, *paraphylakes* must buy at their own expense everything they used except wood (for fuel), chaff (for bedding) and the roof over their heads, and must take no honours (crowns are mentioned) from the village headmen (*OGIS* 527). It is clear that they had been using the force given them against bandits to terrorise and extort from the peasants whom they were supposed to protect.

From the West there is less evidence. But it includes a vivid glimpse of the magistrates of Saepinum in Italy vigorously pursuing runaway slaves and stolen animals (*CIL* 9. 2438), which is enough to make it clear that some type of patrolling was needed and practised in the West too. In the towns we hear occasionally of municipal prisons (e.g. Pliny, *Epp.*10.19). And something of the nature of police work clearly fell to the aediles or their equivalents, albeit on a limited scale. Self-help was undoubtedly more important—nicely illustrated in the curse-tablets of Lydney and Bath, in which the victims of theft sought to win the help of a deity: for example:

> Memorandum to the god Mercury from Saturnina, woman, about linen goods which she has lost—that the thief, whether man or woman, slave or free, have no ease unless and until he brings the aforesaid goods to the aforesaid temple (and Saturnina promises Mercury a third part of the value of the property recovered). (Hassall and Tomlin 1979, 343, no.3).

So also in the great 'chamber-pot' case of Cnidus (*Syll 3*. 780): when, three nights running, rowdies attacked the house of a fellow-citizen, no-one seems to have thought of calling in 'the watch'. Rather, the threatened household defended itself as best it could and, in the course of the affair, a slave let go of a chamber-pot which he was emptying over the heads of the attackers and killed one of them. We might remember also that when St. Paul and Silas were arrested at Philippi in Macedonia, their captors were private citizens who felt threatened by them, not the police—though the magistrates subsequently had Paul and Silas beaten by their men (*Acts of the Apostles* 16,19), which seems to indicate the way in which crime was normally dealt with.

With regard, then, to fire-fighting and policing, the ancient city seems to us to have done a good deal less than it might for its citizens. Nevertheless even here it provided some limited backing for citizens who helped themselves—normally, of course, wealthier citizens who were the only ones in a position to do much.

All civic services cost money. Cities derived income in the first place from local taxation, for which it seems that Roman approval was needed. That approval was readily forthcoming, as far as we know, for taxes which were considered traditional, but approval was only given for new taxes after investigation: the point is illustrated in a letter written by the emperor Vespasian to the Spanish town of Sabora:

> The taxes which you say that you received from the divine Augustus, I retain. If you wish to add new ones, you must approach the governor about them ; for I can institute nothing without a ruling (from him). (*ILS* 6092).

Local taxation might affect the locals' ability to pay Roman taxes. In addition to local taxation, many cities received income from rent of property or interest on loans. Property, and money that could be lent, were normally acquired by bequest. Occasionally we hear of a city buying land to rent: Apollonia in Cyrenaica bought, in conjunction with a private group, a farm which had probably been part of the estate of the last king of Cyrene and which passed on his death in 96 BC to the Roman People (Reynolds and Goodchild 1965). A few cities are known to have derived income from local control of such activities as fishing, like Histria on the west coast of the Black Sea (*SEG* 1.329), or the exchange of local with Roman money, like Pergamum (*OGIS* 484; cf.*IGRR* 3.239 (Lycia)), or the operation of local ferries, like Myra in Lycia (*OGIS* 4302a). No doubt sources of revenue took very many forms.

Where we are informed on the point, it seems that the collection of money from taxpayers, lessees and debtors was normally let to contractors from whom the city's financial magistrates received the money for deposit (cf. the city of Munigua in dispute with its contractor, *AE* 1962, no.288). Accounts-clerks would check it in and out of the treasury. Ultimately these processes were the responsibility of the senior magistrates and the city council—an indication of their evident importance for the city.

No expenditure would be incurred in salaries for magistrates or town councillors, since they served for free; the financial qualification for office (above) should have ensured that they were wealthy enough to do this. And it was increasingly expected that they would meet some, at least, of the expenses of carrying out public business. But some salaried, non-slave assistants were used (e.g. scribes and town criers) and these had to be paid (Pleket 1981). Dio of Prusa refers disparagingly to their posts as among the less satisfying jobs by which the free urban poor might earn a livelihood (*Or.*7.123), though the post of scribe often carried some status. Civic funds were also spent on the purchase and maintenance of public slaves, the maintenance of condemned criminals employed on public works (see Pliny, *Epp.* 10.31, incidentally mentioning the salaries of civically-owned slaves), the travel expenses of those magistrates, councillors and other persons who went abroad on civic business (as envoys, perhaps: Souris 1982), and the cost of materials used in public service—such as tablets for keeping records, brooms and some cleaning materials, materials for the repair of public monuments, fuel for heating water in public baths, oil for rubbing down in baths and gymnasia, animals and other items for public sacrifice, purchase of corn if the local harvest was inadequate etc. This amounted to quite a lot even without any allowance for major maintenance and provision of new buildings.

It is certain that civic incomes often proved insufficient to meet civic needs—much less civic aspirations. Private fortunes had also to be tapped. It was already a feature of the fifth century BC that rich men were required to provide certain resources for their cities under the title of liturgies. This practice continued. At the same time, it came to be the custom that candidates for magistracies promised donations for public purposes. Such donations began as voluntary contributions but hardened into obligatory requirements, so that eventually all magistrates paid a compulsory charge on entry into office (*summa honoraria*). And often all city councillors did the same (cf. Pliny, *Epp.* 10.39.5). These 'donations' were an additional source of income to the city. Indeed, public men apparently came to feel under pressure to give still more, as indicated, for example, in an inscription from the African city of Cirta, where a local notable

> ...set up the statue of the Genius of the People which he promised in respect of the office of triumvir, expending 6,000 sesterces of his own money, and at its dedication gave one denarius to each citizen on the citizen-roll from his own purse and also presented performances in the theatre where additional gifts were thrown to the audience. (Pflaum 1957, no.479).

Moreover, resident aliens came under similar pressure and were formally obliged to perform liturgies in the cities of their residence as well as in those of their origin.

In the event a great deal of public building in the cities was financed privately—often, so the inscriptions indicate, by single donors of great wealth, like the citizen of Spoletium in Italy, who

> ...in respect of the office of quattuorvir held by his son built a basilica from the foundations up, on public land but with his own money. (*ILS* 5532).

Much public building was also funded by the combined efforts of groups of the less wealthy, whose names were less prominently blazoned and whose generosity may be harder to detect. Private donations were made not only for buildings but for many other aspects of public life besides—especially in connection with embassies (when travel expenses might be personally funded by the envoys: Souris 1982), with the corn supply, the oil supply, and the civic cults. Private donors often funded sacrificial dedications, food for feasts, elaborations of old celebrations and introductions of new ones, as is frequently recorded. A good example of such a civic benefactor in this field is an Aphrodisian lady who twice handed out bottles of oil, apparently to all comers and at all hours of the day and night, who sacrificed regularly over several years for the health of the emperors, who banqueted the whole citizen body (what is more with a sit-down meal, not a fork-supper, still less a take-away), who secured for presentation in the theatre of Aphrodisias the best entertainers in Asia and who invited to the festival the citizens of neighbouring cities (*MAMA* 8. 492B). It is clear that there might be citizens whose incomes far outstripped that of the city itself. And some of them, at least, were willing to spend from it quite lavishly for the city. They gained a return in prestige for themselves and for their families and, while it was undoubtedly greatest in their own city, that prestige might spread well beyond it— throughout their province, for instance. Moreover, through the interest of the Roman governors, it might win them Roman citizenship and promotion in the Roman social hierarchy to equestrian and eventually even to senatorial status. Locally too, such generosity helped to counter the potential bitterness of the poor and to restrict or even prevent social unrest.

If on the other hand the city did decide to embark on new building (or reconstruction) with its own funds, it might call on private donations to supplement these and it could also reduce costs by using the corvée system. A good example of this has recently come to light in Syrian Antioch, where a canal was built, with a view especially to an improved water-supply for fullers, by the use of corvées—the citizens in each region of the city provided the labour required on a specific stretch (Van Berchem 1983). The obligation to provide a specified amount of labour annually was included in municipal charters (cf. Gonzalez 1986, ch.83), but we do not often have evidence for the operation of the system. It was also normal for the city to get free oversight of the work, since this was a liturgy. Plutarch (*Mor*.811c) and Dio (*Or*.40.7) describe the tedious unpleasantness that such oversight might involve (in Dio's case in relation to his own donation of a portico). They make it clear that not all overseers are likely to have exerted themselves to the full. On the other hand sometimes supervisors themselves made further donations from their own purses.

This mode of public finance can hardly be regarded as wholly satisfactory. By its very nature it discouraged thoughtful planning. Desirable

schemes were not considered (or were delayed) and necessary repairs were
omitted: inscriptions which record repairs frequently speak of years of neglect set right, which may be exaggeration, but can hardly have been total
invention. By contrast, flashy schemes might absorb the money available,
often, no doubt, because they brought prestige to an individual donor or
satisfied the urge to outdo a neighbouring city. It is perhaps significant that
when governors intervene, or emperors make donations, it is often (albeit
not invariably) for work of a very practical nature on street paving, drains
and baths, to which local inhabitants had not presumably paid adequate
attention.

The same haphazardness—arising largely from the same cause— limited the effectiveness of other benefactions. Inscriptions often record distributions of cash, corn or other goods to the citizens, but nothing that
can have amounted to seriously considered poor-relief. Exceptions, significantly, were the imperially-sponsored alimentary schemes for the upbring-
ing of fixed numbers of girls and boys and also the small number of private
foundations which were modelled on these schemes (Duncan Jones 1982,
ch.7). Most distributions known to us were irregular and were incidental
to particular festivals, both public and private. Moreover, in such distributions the quantities given were often regulated in accordance with the
social status of the recipient in a manner directly contrary to what would
be expected of poor-relief—that is, the eminent received more while the
unimportant needy received less. An example from Syllium in Pamphylia
illustrates the practice: it describes how a rich citizen, in his year of office,
gave

> 20 denarii to each member of the Council, 18 to each member
> of the gerousia and the ekklesia, 2 to each citizen and one to
> each freedman and resident alien. (*IGRR* 3.800).

It is worth noting the implication, incidentally, that this was a city wherein
not all citizens were members of the citizen assembly (the ekklesia).

Plutarch, while maintaining that magistrates had worthwhile tasks, admit-
ted that they must not forget the existence of the Roman officials in their
province and at Rome. Those officials might find reason to object to their
doings and intervene in the city's affairs.

Rome laid certain obligations on city governments: failure to meet
them would undoubtedly cause intervention. The direct tax must be paid
and the city government, or rather a committee of the council (in the East,

called the *decaprotoi*, 'the ten first men'), was held responsible for it. Any
other required levies had also to be raised. We hear a lot about other levies
under the late Republic, but much less thereafter—though some are known:
for instance, two inscriptions, one from Thespiae in Greece and one from
Termessus Maior in Lycia, record civic action in raising soldiers, probably
for Marcus Aurelius' German war (Jones 1971). The tone of these inscriptions seems to reflect the way in which the cities had identified with Rome
and felt an imperial patriotism, though the surprising honours offered to
the volunteers at Thespiae (the privileges of city councillors for themselves
and their parents) could also indicate a certain concern on the part of the
city council to stimulate enough young men of the right, respectable, type
to join up and fulfil their quota.

As we have already seen, it was also desirable to avoid anything suggestive of serious disorder or neglect of Roman interests. The governor's ban
on meetings of the assembly at Prusa illustrates the former point (above).
We may also recall the anxiety of the town clerk of Ephesus over the disorder caused by the silversmiths' protest at St. Paul's teaching ('for we
are in danger to be called in question for this day's uproar', *Acts of the
Apostles* 19.40). At the same time, the way in which the magistrates of
Philippi bundled Paul and Silas out of their city, when they learned that
in beating Paul they had beaten a Roman citizen, suggests anxiety as to
the latter point (*Acts* 16.38). It was, moreover, normally impossible for city
governments to put through new projects without Roman agreement: cities
even came to need permission to erect new buildings (Pliny, *Epp.*10.23-24).

But it was Plutarch's view that cities provoked Roman intervention by
approaching Roman officials when there was neither obligation nor need
to do so. It is interesting to find the emperor Commodus making much
the same point in a letter to Aphrodisias (Reynolds 1982, document 16).
In this case, Aphrodisias had unresolved problems, apparently over money
bequeathed to it for the foundation of festivals, and had asked that the
governor of Asia should visit it to deal with them. Commodus replied
that requests of this kind might easily lead to erosion of civic liberties—he
appears to have thought that the city could have reached a solution without
help. In the end he seems to have arranged for a compromise by which the
city received an advisor in a way which supposedly avoided the risk (gaps
in the text leave the detail unclear).

There can be little doubt that cities were also prone to approach governors and emperors to 'ask permission' for schemes simply in order to

draw attention to actions that demonstrated loyalty—such was the case with civic imperial cults (as distinct from provincial ones, Price 1984). But in Plutarch's view the major reason for unnecessary appeals to the Romans was the bitterness of factional disagreement among local politicians. Undoubtedly, private interests would often be very much involved in civic decisions, making it difficult sometimes to reach a proper conclusion. Thus at Aphrodisias it is quite likely that some of the problems behind the correspondence with Commodus had arisen because one or more of the local politicians had diverted the incomes of bequests (which should have been building up capital to fund the celebration of the festivals for which they had been bequeathed) to provide for the more immediate satisfaction of the population with large distributions of free oil (Reynolds 1982a, document 62). The popularity of such a distribution presumably made it difficult for fellow politicians to attack it. In fact it seems likely that the stimulus to have the matter set right came from non-citizen groups, free of civic entanglements, notably the synod of Dionysiac Artists, who wanted the chance to compete for the prizes to be offered at the festivals (Reynolds 1982a, document 57).

Another telling example of an appeal to a governor, behind which we may see a similar difficulty, comes from Pisidian Antioch in the reign of Domitian (*MW* 464). Here, after a bad harvest, shortage of grain had pushed up its market-price intolerably. It was to the financial advantage of those local office-holders who owned the bulk of what harvest there was (since they owned the land) to hoard grain until the maximum possible price could be obtained. On the other hand, there were probably men of moderate means on the city council who would be hard-hit by this, as would the poor. And it was certainly to the advantage of all to avoid bread riots—since the violence of ordinary people, when roused, could constitute a real threat even to the civic elite, as we have seen (cf.Dio *Or.* 46.11). Riots were also liable to bring in the Roman governor. Apparently the city council failed to reach an agreed decision in this impasse and therefore appealed to the governor. The governor required owners to declare their stocks and the needs of their own households, and to sell the difference at a price fixed on a reasonable basis. All this, one might have thought, the city council could have done on its own initiative—but, it seems, no one locally was able or willing to thwart the interests of the rich and powerful.

But the elite was not a monolith. Outright feuding among elite families could be extraordinarily bitter and marked by unscrupulous attempts to get rid of an opponent by accusing him to the Romans of crimes very serious in Roman eyes. The case of Claudius Aristion of Ephesus provides an example: jealous of the popularity he had won by public benefactions, his enemies suborned an informer to lay charges which brought him to trial before Trajan (Pliny, *Epp*.6.31.3). Dio of Prusa represents his opponents in Prusa as capable of almost anything (e.g. *Or*.43): and we may suppose that to accuse an enemy to the Romans was a fairly common ploy. Sometimes, civic groupings cloaked their local enmities under the cover of Roman factional affiliations, especially, but not only, during periods of Roman civil war (Bowersock 1984, 179, 184). Such men were eager to bring in their Roman friends to their own advantage. And local disputes could erupt into violence, as we have seen with the case of the chamber-pot at Cnidus, which may have had a political aspect. When local feelings ran high the weaker side might appeal to Rome in the belief that there was no hope of justice for them in a local court—that may be why the Cnidian case came to Augustus.

Plutarch was surely talking sense. But it is also true that the emperors had no hesitation in issuing, without consultation, decrees that affected and bound the cities. A case in point is the series of imperial decrees which gave immunity from various civic obligations to doctors, teachers, rhetors, and eventually philosophers (Bowersock 1969, 30-42; Nutton 1971). On the face of it, these decrees were designed to encourage those who carried on and extended the Greek cultural tradition, in which the cities took pride. But, in the long run, they tended to reduce awkwardly the total number of those persons who contributed to each city's financial needs. In consequence the numbers in each exempt category had later to be limited. In addition, emperors might order and governors carry out inspections of civic papers and accounts. In fact, if they saw fit, they might and did override a city's right to handle its own affairs (Pliny, *Epp*.10.47-48).

Financial mismanagement, or suspicion of it, was a common cause of such Roman intervention in cities. Civic bankruptcy was something that emperors could not risk. From the time of Trajan we begin to hear of occasional missions given to governors, of whom Pliny in Bithynia-Pontus is the best-known example, to investigate the finances and management of the cities of a province. At about the same time we also begin to hear of the appointment to individual cities, at first a few but subsequently an increasing number, of financial overseers with the title of *curator reipublicae* or *logistes*. Pliny's letters from his province to Trajan (*Epp*.10) make it clear that the main trouble there—and perhaps very often elsewhere—was not so much a real shortage of money as extravagant and careless use of what there was and, on occasion, of the assets that produced this wealth. Lax administration, which had allowed convicts to get onto the civic payroll at Nicomedeia (*Epp*.10.31), is one of many indications of the inadequacies that might occur in civic government. Large expenditure on ill-devised building schemes is another (*Epp*.10.37 for Nicomedeia, 39 for Nicaea and

Claudiopolis). Yet another is unnecessary expenditure on annual and essentially ceremonial embassies to the emperor at Rome and the governor of a neighbouring province (*Epp*.10.43, Byzantium).

We may supplement Pliny's information from other sources. An inscription from Caere, just north of Rome, preserves an interchange between the city's magistrates and its *curator reipublicae* (*ILS* 5918a). In this case, the city council had agreed to allow use of a small piece of publicly-owned land by a private person who wished to build a shrine. Submitting their decision to their curator, the magistrates explained that the land at issue brought in no income and was not likely to do so. Our suspicion that one reason for the curator's appointment was earlier failure of the city council to check such facts of its own volition can be sharpened by the contents of an unpublished inscription from Aphrodisias, probably of the early first century AD. There the council and the people had passed a decree that a public funeral and a tomb constructed on public property within the city boundary (a very rare honour) should be given, when the time came, to a local notable (the reason for the honour is lost to us). The honorand added to his kudos, we learn, by getting up in the Council chamber and asserting that he would not accept that part of the honour which would deprive the city of income (for the site was almost certainly let out for rent as a shop/workshop); he offered instead a similar and no doubt adjacent piece of property of his own. Citizens of that kind were clearly not always available to prevent follies; and it is not even certain how careful were the investigations made as a result of the cities' applications for permission to build (above). Waste, inefficiency and no doubt corruption continued - and that is probably why more and more curators were appointed. For the most part we only hear of them in the inscriptions in which cities thanked them for their help, or in which their careers were recorded, as on their tombstones. It is therefore worth drawing attention to the one curator on whose work we have detailed information, M.Ulpius Appuleius Eurycles of Aezani in Phrygia (*OGIS* 504-7 and Reynolds 1982a, document 57), who appears to have brought a very conscientious and sensible approach to the problems that he faced at Aphrodisias.

Rome, then, made substantial demands on the cities—and, as she saw fit, interfered with their handling of their affairs. But it is perhaps fair to say that she also gave to them. She gave more than the long-term advantages of the general Roman peace and the comparatively easy communications she ensured throughout the Mediterranean world and to some extent beyond it. Emperors passed long hours listening to civic embassies and seeking solutions to problems. Emperors and members of the imperial family sometimes actually held civic magistracies (exercising the duties through a distinguished local) to honour the cities in which they held them. At such a time especially (though also at other times) emperors spent money directly on them (Millar 1977, 363-463). They were especially generous after disasters, which sometimes created havoc beyond the means of the citizens to repair quickly, as in Asia, after the major earthquake of AD 17 (Tacitus, *Ann*.2.47), and in Cyrene, after the destructive Jewish Revolt of AD 115 (Fraser and Applebaum 1951). They might also be attracted by practical schemes for improvement—Pliny represents Trajan as likely to consider a donation when he reported his idea for a canal to link Nicomedeia to the sea (*Epp*.10.42). Such plans may often have received imperial subsidy as a result of reports from a governor—so perhaps when a governor acted as Trajan's agent in the construction of a Roman bath at Cyrene (Reynolds 1959). But unofficial approaches may often have lain behind them—an approach from Claudius' Coan doctor Xenophon for instance was behind his grant of immunity to Cos (Tacitus, *Ann*.12.61). And when Trajan made a gift to Aphrodisias with money bequeathed to him by an Aphrodisian citizen, using the deceased's brother as his agent (Reynolds 1982a, document 55), it is tempting to suppose that the brother had come up with the particular proposal (which perhaps involved representation of a story from the Aeneas cycle and was therefore distinctly relevant to Rome) after the emperor had expressed a desire to spend this Aphrodisian money locally.

The appointments of curators, and of governors with commissions like that of Pliny, have been used as part of an argument that enthusiasm for city government and the vigour of the city system waned, already a little in the first century AD and with gathering force in the second. The issue is confused by the fact that extensive public building and other apparent signs of civic vigour in this period coincide with evidence for unwillingness within the governing classes to undertake all their public obligations. It is true that eventually—by the fourth century, without doubt—civic office did lose its attractions and become compulsory. But we are less sure as to precisely how this situation came about, and when; and much of the earlier evidence seems to be equivocal (Garnsey 1974). We have seen that appointments of curators do not necessarily imply a shortage of money—or of enthusiasm for civic affairs —in the cities in which they were appointed. In the same way, the provision made in the late first century charter of the city of Malaca in Spain (*ILS* 6089, ch. 51) for a situation in which no candidates, or too few, came forward at an election, does not necessarily mean that there was any reason to expect that this would actually happen, except in very abnormal circumstances—as for instance in a war (and there had just been the civil war of AD 68/9 to remind draftsmen of war's effects) or a plague.

Such a situation did arise occasionally, but to our knowledge always in abnormal situations, as at Cyrene. There, after the destruction of the Jewish Revolt of AD 115, a list of the names of eponymous priests, almost certainly from the reign of Hadrian, twice names the city in place of a person: we may therefore suppose that in those two years there was no candidate for the office so that the city itself had to undertake its expenses and ceremonial (Smith and Porcher 1964, no.10). It has recently been argued, on the basis of a detailed study of the electoral advertisements called *programmata* at Pompeii (examples in *ILS* 6398-6438), that by AD 79, when the city was overwhelmed by lava, there were no more than two men standing for election as senior magistrates each year, which was precisely the number needed, so that elections were a farce (Franklin 1980). But even if the argument is accepted (and its archaeological basis is not quite free of difficulties), a reduction in the number of candidates in Pompeii at this date may be explained as the result of abnormal losses in the serious earthquake of AD 62—again something that was quite local and might have been quite temporary. When men sought to avoid liturgies or office in the second century AD it was, sometimes at least, because they had a right to immunity (in itself, prestigious), as was the case with the Aphrodisian resident at Smyrna whose right to exemption from the liturgies of the other cities and of the province of Asia was upheld by Trajan (Reynolds, 1982a, document 14). But there can be no doubt that unwillingness to serve became something of an issue in the course of the second century AD. It is also clear that some made considerable efforts to make others accept duties that both preferred to avoid. Some city councillors may already have been compelled to serve by Pliny's time (*Epp.*10.13, where many believe that the text should read *inviti*, unwilling, rather than *invitati*, invited). If so, there is apparently conflicting evidence from Prusa where the city wanted a larger council than it had and persuaded Trajan to allow an increase of 100 members (Dio, *Or.* 45.7). But by the second half of the second century Marcus and Verus certainly wrote of some magistrates as serving under compulsion (*Digest* 50.1.38.6). And under Severus some cities of Asia petitioned for permission to include Jews in their city council—they would hardly have accepted men who could not participate in the pagan rituals of the city unless there had been serious difficulty in finding recruits (for additional evidence, see Garnsey 1974). Of course we do not know how many cities were feeling the problem—it may have been a small number only. Nevertheless the problem existed and needs explanation.

It may be important that in many cities the composition of the governing class had been modified over the years. Old families had sometimes disappeared. Their heirs had sometimes gone abroad, since clever young men were certainly being attracted to display their talents in more sophisticated and rewarding settings than most cities offered. So, for example, the elder Seneca left Corduba and Martial left Bilbilis for Rome. If such men returned home it might only be late in life. Others wanted office in the provincial organisations and, although not lost to their cities, they might spend less of their time and money at home than their fathers had done. Yet others sought the status of Roman *eques* and the offices in the Roman public service for which that status qualified them. They might come home after a little time in this employment, but a number stayed away for longish periods. A very few reached the Roman Senate, which involved a much more serious separation from home. A senator might keep in touch with home, as the younger Pliny did, help his city and its citizens, visit occasionally. That is perhaps the normal pattern of behaviour for the first generation senator; but the evidence suggests that the link grew weaker generation by generation. In any case, a senator needed to withdraw a considerable amount of his income to maintain the dignity of his status in Italy, so that his city certainly lost not only his services but also much money that he might have spent on it had he stayed—for a small city such a loss could be very serious indeed. A friendly senator might be useful as a patron of his city—but it is doubtful whether this was always effective compensation.

Further, some of the families which stayed died out, as in cities such as Cyrene in the first century AD or Aphrodisias in the second. In those cities we know a little about some family histories, thanks to inscriptions. Two indications of the problem are the incidence of adoptions within the governing class (e.g. *CIG* 5132, 2748), and, very particularly at Aphrodisias, the number of occasions when very great wealth had come into the hands of women, presumably in default of a male heir (for an example *MAMA* 8. 492B). There is, however, little reason to suppose that either city was seriously short of willing candidates for office until Cyrene was stricken by war (above).

Where old families withdrew or died out, new ones came forward. At Pompeii some of these seem to have been descendants of freed slaves (Castrén 1975). At Cyrene in the middle of the first century one of the magistrates called *nomophylakes*, engaged in part in archival duties, was a Jew, to judge by his name, presumably an apostate since he joined in a religious dedication (*SEG* 20. 737 cf. Applebaum 1964). At Aphrodisias, probably in the early third century, nine of the city councillors belonged to a group described as 'god-fearers', closely associated with the local synagogue (Reynolds and Tannenbaum, 1986). Further, there is some recently collected evidence for more tradesmen and craftsmen among town councillors than had been thought (Pleket 1984). We do not know what proportion they constituted. To men of such backgrounds the status accorded to those who participated in city government continued to be very attractive. That status was enhanced by the emergence of legal privilege (better treatment before the law, lighter punishments) for those classed as 'more honourable' (*honestiores*), as city councillors were (Garnsey 1970). It seems, however, likely that, on the whole, they will not have been as wealthy as the sons of the older families who possessed large inherited estates. In fact there are indications of this in the evidence of relative poverty among some members of city councils (Garnsey 1974, 233-4). And a striking new inscription of the second century AD from Nimes attests loans advanced by a rich freedman to local magistrates in order to enable them to meet the expenses of their offices (*AE* 1982, no.681). At the same time the Romans were certainly not slackening their demands on city governments, while within cities there was an intensification of the pressures on individual members of the governing class to give more. Vigorous rivalries between cities played some part in this, as the level of what any self-respecting city thought necessary rose, and rose again. But, for all that, the city system seems still to have had a lot of life in it, perhaps until the later third century (Garnsey 1974).

The city was a stage on which the civic elite displayed and enjoyed the incomes which it derived principally from the land of the territory—displayed them in public munificence and public service, but also in private lives both by indulgence in material splendour and by the maintenance of their cultural traditions. The cities provided opportunities for education, both by private teachers and by civic arrangements for the training of boys and young men (in the East mainly associated with the gymnasia). Learning was further encouraged by the immunities from civic obligations which were offered to doctors, teachers and scholars (Nutton 1971). They offered opportunities for visiting speakers to harangue audiences at high-brow and low-brow levels alike. They also organised competitions in literary exercises and musical attainments as well as in athletics. Other skills might also be included from time to time—e.g. at Aphrodisias in the third century AD there was a public competition for sculptors (*MAMA* 8.519). The very various origins of those who made their names at Rome as writers, speakers and scholars is testimony to the availability of education in cities all over the empire. Some cities were famous for particular studies as Athens was for philosophy and Cos for medicine. Very many reveal the cultural interests and aspirations of their citizens in their inscriptions. Thus at the rather remote city of Oenoanda in Lycia an enthusiast had the works of Epicurus inscribed on a public building for the improvement of his fellow-citizens (Hall 1979 on the man ; Smith 1978, 1979 on the inscription). And although few of the surviving funerary verses in city cemeteries could claim much literary merit, they do, nevertheless, indicate a remarkably widespread urge to versify in the great traditions of Greek and of Roman culture (cf.Horsfall 1985 for an interesting example).

For others the city offered means of livelihood which might enable them to rise in wealth and status. In inscriptions, supplemented by a few literary sources (notably Dio, *Or.* 7.105f.), a great range of occupations is attested—from the scribe or scrivener to the porter in the docks and market-places. Prominent are men in the service trades (bakers, cooks, shopkeepers, for instance) and producers of luxuries (goldsmiths, silversmiths, purple dyers, mosaicists). But a considerable number were producing goods which were useful if not so very glamorous—masons, woodworkers, leather-workers, cloth and clothing workers, potters and the like. Most of their work was directed no doubt to supplying the local market, in which the demands of the very rich may have predominated, but were not alone. Some families, like Dio's Euboean huntsmen, doubtless met most of their needs through domestic production— women spinning and weaving, men curing and cutting skins, cutting timber and making wooden implements—some of which might serve instead of pottery. But the quite frequent incidence of 'rag-pickers' (who included second-hand clothes dealers) would tend to imply the existence of less well-to-do customers. And indeed Dio envisages the urban poor as buying all they need and notes the difficulty they will have in earning enough to meet the cost (*Or.*7.105-6). In some towns—ports, for instance—there would always be visitors to provide for as well. In others visitors came on festival occasions or at assizes. In some cities there was production for export. Such production tends only to show itself when a local product acquired an empire-wide reputation, as did the linen of Tarsus, the wool of Tarentum or Mutina and the glass of Alexandria. There were, indeed, 'backwoods' cities— country towns in which export and import of goods was on a very small scale. But we may, even so, envisage the city in the Roman world not simply as a 'consumer city', living essentially off its countryside, but as a place where some of the products of the territory were processed into exportable goods (Hopkins 1978), and where some of the products of other territories were available for those who could afford to buy them.

Just a little can be said of the lives of the tradesmen, craftsmen and merchants in some cities. There is literary evidence for Prusa (Dio, *Or.*7) and epigraphic evidence from many sites. These can sometimes be supplemented by material remains, as of potteries at Arretium (Peacock 1982, 119-122) and of fulleries at Pompeii, where there are also some painted illustrations of shops and of work in progress (Etienne 1974). Production was in small units—one man often working alone or with his son or with an employee, even perhaps a slave, or two. Many men used a trade designation, apparently with pride. Some built monuments (usually for their tombs) which display moderate, even substantial wealth. In many cities tradesmen formed trade associations. These were primarily for cult and social occasions (feasts play a major part in the evidence, and provision of burial for poorer members another). However, it is hardly possible to believe that no one ever talked shop with his fellow-members. The incident of the silversmiths at Ephesus (above) shows in any case that members might be conscious of their common interests and press for them as a group. At Pompeii the trade associations are known to have supported particular candidates in elections (Etienne 1974): for example:

> The fruiterers ask you to make M.Holconius Priscus aedile. (*ILS* 6411c).

And,

> The muleteers ask for C.Julius Polybius as aedile.(*ILS* 6412a).

In fact such associations were integrated into the city system. Inscriptions from Ephesus show that they might be allotted space in public buildings— for offices, perhaps also for markets (*I.Eph.*2076-82). In the West, as we have seen, they might provide fire-services for the community. In the East they are sometimes recorded as making public dedications—as the 'ragpickers' did to Augustus at Cos (*NSRC* 466). In some cities (e.g. Aphrodisias, unpublished inscriptions) we know that they might have blocks of reserved seats in amphitheatres, stadia and theatres. They therefore participated in their city's public occasions as associations. And in this they are closely analogous with associations of the well-to-do in the cities—those for older men (*gerousiae*), for youths (*ephebes*) and for young men (*neoi*) (Oliver 1941; Jones 1940, 220-26).

Trade associations were thus integrated into civic life and, though strictly controlled by Roman legislation (for the Romans feared their potential for disorder), they provided groupings which eased the social inequalities of the ancient city for many citizens of low status. Some members, whose standing was inadequate for civic office, satisfied talents for organisation and administration as officers of their associations. At group dinners many members could enjoy amenities which they could not have afforded as individuals. In time of stress the poorer could hope for help from their fellows. There is good evidence that help was given in the matter of funerals and tombs, whose importance should not be underestimated (Waltzing 1895). In the West the imperial cult provided public positions under the titles of *seviri* and *Augustales* for the most successful freedmen residents and citizens, who would often have been members of the trade associations. In office these men carried out (at some financial cost to themselves) public rituals, which brought them prestige. Subsequently they were recognised as members of a group accorded honours above those of ordinary citizens on public occasions. If they played their cards well—which meant, in essence, spending substantial sums on public entertainments and projects—they could expect that their sons would have the opportunity of holding civic office as accepted members of the elite.

While the city pervaded the lives of its urban population, for which it provided a whole context, its relations with its rural territory were rather more ambivalent. Many landowners doubtless exploited their landed estates, and their work-force, without mercy. Some were at least interested in applying technical information, acquired through the cultural media of the towns, if only to preserve their investments and maximise their profits (Columella and Pliny, *NH* 15.47 for instance). At the same time cities might ignore their rural citizens until they wanted money from them, as Dio casually indicates in his account of the Euboean huntsmen (*Or.* 7). But for some inhabitants of the territory, at least, urban amenities—markets, opportunities for paid work and for participation in public entertainment—were accessible.

Indeed, villages sometimes had reserved blocks of seats in amphitheatres and the like (for civic participation in a civic festival, see the remarkable new inscription from Oenoanda in Lycia, outlined by Wörrle 1987). We cannot properly estimate how often most peasants went into town. Their presence is sometimes noted on specific occasions, as when a priestess of Artemis at Cyrene invited the girls of the territory as well as of the urban centre to a feast which probably celebrated Trajan's second Dacian victory (*SEG* 26.1826), though that, in itself, suggests that it was not always so. The better-off country men might come in regularly, but surely not all. To Dio's Euboean huntsmen the city was unfamiliar and alarming, a place where a man might perhaps hope to get paid employment and earn his living in a crisis (but, in this case, failed to find work), a place from which autocratic and unrealistic demands might issue—best avoided; they had no need even of its markets—they produced most of what they wanted themselves and could get the rest from a village.

One more category of citizen deserves mention. Cities were men's worlds; but a woman citizen, daughter of a citizen mother and father, had some recognised functions, other than that of bearing the next generation. These seem to have been mainly—even exclusively—for the well-to-do. Women held office as priestesses in the public cults of the city and performed certain rituals. At Cyrene, for instance, the priestess of Artemis was named alongside the priest of Apollo, who held the city's most important priesthood (*CIG* 5130). At Aphrodisias there were not only priestesses alongside the priests of Aphrodite but also a category of girls named 'flower-bearers' (*MAMA* 8.574): they presumably carried flowers in processions for Aphrodite. Everywhere women played a part in imperial cult, often alongside their husbands, but not only so, as we have seen at Aphrodisias (above). Women are also attested making public donations: in so doing they perhaps often stood in for a deceased father or husband, or for an infant son. They could not be rewarded with offices, but did receive formal titles (mother of the city, daughter of the city, for instance)—and sometimes these were the titles of office, presumably when the office was a sinecure or wholly ceremonial—perpetual gymnasiarch, for a lady who had set up a fund to buy oil for a gymnasium for instance, or *stephanephoros*, a priestly title sometimes held by annual priests who gave their names to the year in which they held office, as at Aphrodisias, (they clearly spent money on sacrifices, but perhaps did little else). The women so far described would normally be of the governing class. Lower down the social scale—but still among the well-to-do—women are sometimes found as patronesses of associations (whether trade associations or purely cult associations). A case in point is the patroness of the 'club' of 'lovers of learning' within the synagogue community at Aphrodisias (Reynolds and Tannenbaum 1986, face 'a'). It is at any rate clear that the city, or the subsidiary organisations within it, offered some recognition and some part for a woman of means to play. A poor woman was perhaps not so much worse off in this respect than a poor man.

In a short space it is not possible to cover every aspect of the life of ancient cities or to use all the very various kinds of scattered evidence about it. Enough has perhaps been said to indicate the important place held by cities in the Roman world, both from the Roman viewpoint and from that of their citizens. And we can make a case for the continuing vigour of cities as institutions (whatever may have happened in particular instances) certainly up to the end of the second century AD.

Administration, Urbanisation and Acculturation in the Roman West

W.S. HANSON

When the Roman state expanded into western Europe it encountered peoples who for the most part lacked an urban lifestyle, at least in a form which the Romans would have readily acknowledged. This is in marked contrast to the situation in the eastern Mediterranean where Rome came into contact with civilisations with a long-established urban tradition. For most of the inhabitants of the Greco-Roman world, the possession and exercise of the citizenship of a city which was in some sense self-governing was an essential prerequisite if a person was to consider himself civilised. More importantly for our present purposes Roman local administration was based on urban centres, or rather city-states with an urban focus. The questions then arise, how did Rome deal administratively with areas which lacked urban forms and in what way did this affect the nature and extent of the empire in the West?

The simple answer to the first question is that Rome established towns. This could be done most easily by directly planting colonies of Roman citizens in recently-conquered territory. But there were not sufficient citizens available, or willing, to be shipped off and settled in new lands, for population pressure does not seem to have been one of the major factors influencing the expansion of the Roman empire. Such direct action was not, therefore, really feasible as the main process of urban formation. Nonetheless such cities were established quite widely. Even in the remote province of Britain we see the foundation of a colony of Roman citizens at Colchester as early as six years after conquest. But this foundation—like most such settlements—was intended primarily to house legionary veterans who were to serve both as a military reserve and as a model of the Roman lifestyle for the indigenous population. At the same time settlement at Colchester was, for the legionaries, a reward for their service to the state.

It was not possible to establish sufficient citizen colonies throughout newly-conquered territory. The alternative was to create towns by indirect means, by encouraging the development of urban communities with peregrine status. In other words, the Romans could ensure that the indigenous population developed an urban lifestyle for itself. This seems to have been the strategy most usually favoured by Rome: we must therefore consider exactly when, where and how it was employed.

Where the Roman advance met with resistance, as was frequently the case, the normal procedure was conquest followed by military occupation. It seems logical to assume that the formal takeover of control by civilians would have come about after the departure of the troops, since the presence of an army of occupation tends by its very nature to usurp any civilian authority. Of course the military may very well have worked through any surviving native infrastructure. Indeed, it would have been in the best interests of Rome so to do in order to ensure that natives who were suitably accustomed to Roman ways would be available to assume full authority one day. It is perfectly possible that authority was in some cases transferred without there being any immediately recognisable physical manifestation of that transferral, as, apparently, in the Danubian provinces (see below). But, given the association in Roman thinking between administration and urbanisation, it seems probable that the Romans tended to look towards developing urban centres as the natural foci of authority. They will have expected to see the speedy development of the physical trappings of Roman-style administration, particularly the construction of a forum-basilica complex. But where towns were built directly over an abandoned military base, as seems to have been the case in Britain at Wroxeter and Exeter, there must have been some time-lag in the change, for the construction of urban buildings could not commence until the army had moved and its fortress had been demolished.

If on the other hand the Romans were welcomed, or at least not actively resisted, the handing over of authority may have been more rapid. This seems to have been the case in Britain at Canterbury and perhaps Chelmsford, if the latter was indeed the capital of the Trinovantes (Wacher 1974, 178-202). The rapid urban development at Verulamium in the territory of the Catuvellauni, who led the opposition to Rome, seems out of place in this context, but this may reflect the differential treatment of different factions within the tribe, for pro-Roman elements are attested, such as that represented by Adminius who fled as a suppliant to Rome (Wacher 1974, 203).

In similar vein we see the development of urban forms of settlement in the territory of the friendly or client king Cogidubnus even before it had been formally annexed and brought under direct Roman administrative control. Such differences in treatment are probably reflected in the graded status of *civitates*: those formally allied with Rome (*foederatae*), those nominally free (*liberae*) and those which officially paid tribute (*stipendiariae*). These variations are best attested in Gaul, where to some extent at least they mirror the different attitudes of the tribal groups towards Caesar—the Remi and Lingones had been rewarded with the status of *civitates foederatae*; the Leuci, Nervii, Treveri and Suessiones were made *civitates liberae*; the Morini, Menapii and Ambiani all became *civitates stipendiariae* (Wightman 1985, 55-6).

It was for administrative purposes that newly-created provinces were divided up into distinct communities with clearly- definable boundaries: in some cases in Spain and Dalmatia we even have surviving boundary stones (*CIL* II, 460; *AE* 1976, 273; Wilkes 1969, 456-9). These *civitates* were most easily defined on the basis of the indigenous tribal structure: a pattern readily identifiable in western Spain (Pliny *NH* 3.3.27-8), Gaul (Tacitus *Annals* 3.44) and Britain (Ptolemy *Geog.* 2.3). It should be stressed, however, that the Romans were not averse to adjusting the divisions for their own administrative convenience. Thus, in Britain the *civitates* of the Belgae and Regnenses appear to have been created from a larger tribal grouping, the Atrebates (Rivet 1977, 161-4). In Gaul similar adjustments are known— the Tungri seem to be an amalgamation of three or more smaller groups (Drinkwater 1983, 93-4; Wightman 1985, 53). In Spain the tribal confederations of the Vaccaei and Cantabri do not seem to have been recognised by any Roman administrative division (Mackie 1983a, 21-2 and 30-31).

In most cases the administrative focus of these *civitates* was a town. For convenience a single centre was preferred and there has been considerable debate over the factors which influenced the choice of location for the foundation of a town where none previously existed. In Britain the presence of a Roman fort at a particular site has long been considered significant in this respect (Webster 1966). But more recently the primary importance of the pre-Roman settlement pattern has been asserted (Millett 1984). In all probability, however, both factors had a part to play. The existence of a pre-Roman settlement nucleus would seem to facilitate the establishment of an urban centre, while the potential social and economic attraction of living outside the walls of even a small military establishment should not be underestimated as a stimulus to settlement agglomeration. The statistics for Britain would seem to support this view. Of the 14 securely known sites of *civitas* capitals, four (Chichester, Exeter, Wroxeter and Carmarthen) succeeded Roman military establishments, five (Canterbury, Verulamium, Silchester, Dorchester and Leicester) were preceded by native Iron-age settlement, two (Cirencester and Winchester) show evidence of both Roman military and native precursors, while the evidence from the remaining three (Caistor by Norwich, Caerwent and Aldborough) is uncertain (Burnham 1986, 193-4). It should be stressed, however, that since the number of examples involved is quite small any new discoveries could have a dramatic effect on the present balance apparent in the figures. The independent importance of the military factor has been asserted for Gaul also (Wightman 1985, 49), but there the pre-Roman settlement pattern appears to have been the major determinant in the location of towns, constrained or amended by the new communications system within which, of course, military sites were nodal (Drinkwater 1985, 49).

The attraction of junctions in the newly-established network of communications was as important in stimulating the foundation of administrative centres as it was in promoting other urban settlements. Parallel factors can be seen at work: according to a recent survey of Romano-British 'small towns', 36 per cent could claim military origins and 37 per cent could claim Iron Age precursors, though the last figure includes sites with evidence of both. The remaining 27 per cent were of uncertain origin. However, position within the main network of communications appears to have been a major factor in the foundation and subsequent development of most of the sites considered (Burnham 1986).

One of the most intriguing questions, however, concerns the way in which 'administrative' towns came into existence. Did the Roman authorities enforce their construction, merely encourage it, or leave it entirely to the whim of the indigenous population? It has long been assumed that the Romans would have instituted some formal programme of urban foundation, given the importance of towns as administrative centres. The current trend, however, perhaps in reaction to previously-held views, is to emphasise the generally *laissez-faire* attitude of the Romans and look to external factors as the main stimulus to urban development—in particular the desire of the native aristocracy to emulate Roman ways.

It was thought that the Romans forcibly removed the population from local centres, such as hill-forts, to newly-created towns, a view fostered in particular by reference to the recorded treatment of tribes in Spain. Concerned that they might take advantage of refuge in the mountains after their defeat, Augustus ordered the Asturians and Cantabrians to occupy and cultivate the area where his camp had stood:

> After this we were able to rely on the loyalty of the Spaniards
> and uninterrupted peace ensued as a result both of their nat-

ural disposition for the arts of peace and also of the wise
measures taken by Caesar. Fearing the confidence inspired in
them by their mountain refuges, he ordered them to occupy
and cultivate the area of the plain where his camp had been.
He urged that the council of the nation should be held there
and the place regarded as their capital. (Florus 2.33).

Similarly, Dio states that Agrippa forced the Cantabrians to come down
from their fortresses and live in the plains (Dio 54.11.5). But both of these
accounts seem to refer to actions taken for reasons of security immediately
after campaigns. They are not, therefore, entirely trustworthy records of
overall Roman policy towards urban foundation in such areas. Indeed, Dio
does not even specify the nature of the settlement involved.

When we turn to the archaeological evidence, instead of finding that
native centres were always abandoned when new towns were founded nearby, there are some indications that the two could have been occupied simultaneously for some time. The gradual transference of population from pre-
Roman to Roman centres is hardly commensurate with a policy of forcible
expulsion. For example, we see the construction of Romanised buildings in
the large *oppidum* of the Aedui at Mont Beuvray before the site was eventually eclipsed by the new town at Autun (Drinkwater 1983, 131). A similar
situation may be evidenced at Bagendon in the territory of the Dobunni
in England. Occupation there certainly continued for some time after the
foundation of the nearby fort and *vicus* at Cirencester (Wacher 1974, 30-1),
but since the earliest phases at Bagendon are now seen to be of Roman
date (Swann 1975, 59-61), that occupation may well have continued after
the fort was in turn replaced by the *civitas* capital. The more widespread
this pattern proves to be, the more significant it becomes, for the gradual
transferral of populations from pre-Roman to Roman centres does not look
like a crude policy of forcible expulsion by Rome. Moreover, the very fact
that there were areas under Roman administration where towns were not
established (see below) would seem to support the view that a consistent
policy of enforcing town foundation was not followed.

To go to the opposite extreme and suggest that the process of urbanisation was left entirely to chance, however, is difficult to substantiate. There
can be little doubt that the desire to emulate Roman ways among the native
aristocracy was an important factor in the successful spread of the Roman
empire. The abundant epigraphic record of public munificence in towns
provides ample indication of the involvement and commitment of the local
elite (Duncan-Jones 1985; Drinkwater 1979, 238-9). It is true that much of
the evidence comes from the North African provinces, which had already
been long exposed to Mediterranean culture as a result of Carthaginian and

Greek colonisation. But the principle is also well attested in Spain, Gaul
and the Danubian provinces. Even in north Britain we see the construction
of part of a theatre at Brough-on-Humber, probably the *civitas* capital of
the Parisii, at the expense of a local magistrate (*RIB* 707). Similarly, at
Metz in Gaul a swimming pool and courtyard were paid for by a local notable (*CIL* 13.4324). But there is no reason to believe that the process was
not actively encouraged by Rome. Indeed, there is clear evidence of direct
Roman encouragement of such urban development in some cases, though,
where an imperial power is concerned, the line between encouragement and
compulsion may be a thin one. The process of urbanisation and Romanisation had already begun in Germany in AD 9, but went astray, according
to Dio, when Varus tried to speed up the pace of change:

> Soldiers of the Roman army were wintering there and towns
> were being founded: the natives were adapting themselves to
> orderly Roman ways and were becoming accustomed to hold-
> ing markets and were meeting in peaceful assemblies. They
> had not, however, forgotten their ancestral habits, their na-
> tive customs, their old life of independence or the power de-
> rived from weapons. Hence, so long as they were learning
> these customs gradually and by the way, one might say, under
> careful surveillance, they were not disturbed by the change in
> the manner of their life and were becoming different without
> knowing it. But when Quintilius Varus became governor in
> Germany and thus administered the affairs of these peoples,
> he strove to change them more rapidly. (Dio 56.18.2-3).

Revolt ensued and Rome suffered the Varian disaster.

But by far the most famous and most explicit evidence of such Roman 'encouragement' is the testimony of Tacitus concerning the actions of
Agricola while he was governor of Britain:

> He encouraged individuals and assisted communities to build
> temples, fora and private houses. He praised the energetic
> and scolded the slack. Competition for honour took the place
> of compulsion. And he had the sons of the leading men ed-
> ucated in the liberal arts. He expressed a preference for the
> natural talents of the British over the trained abilities of the
> Gauls, so that those who used to reject the Roman tongue
> now coveted its eloquence. Thence our manner of dress be-
> came fashionable and the toga was often to be seen. (Tacitus,
> *Agr.*21).

Tacitus, in moralising mood, proceeds to describe the decline which he
thinks to have followed as Britons adopted not only good old Roman practices but also more dubious ones. Yet he stresses and approves the conscious
Romanisation of the Britons by Agricola, which is presented as a deliberate

set of actions on the part of the Roman governor. It is worth noting that the passage also states that compulsion was not necessary, from which one may reasonably infer that compulsion was, nevertheless, a possibility. And it is unreasonable to argue that Agricola's actions were simply an individual initiative, for they accord with other contemporary Flavian actions on the extension of citizenship and the development of education in the provinces (Hanson 1987, 73-82). Indeed, the fact that we seem to see phases of urban development on a regional scale under particular regimes, such as under the Flavians and under Hadrian, suggests that a broader policy of urban development was applied by certain emperors (Sherwin-White 1973, 252-3).

There is also archaeological evidence which is strongly suggestive of some overall policy. The very form of the *civitas* capitals smacks of official involvement. One of the most striking features of these towns is their street pattern (Fig.1). Though not necessarily conforming to any standard measurements, a rectilinear grid of streets was the norm which, on analogy with colonies, would tend to imply deliberate foundation at a particular point in time under the guidance of a single powerful authority. Of all the elements of urban topography, the street pattern tends to be the most enduring and least likely to undergo major change as a result of unplanned organic development. The contrast between the grid-iron pattern of streets in colonies and *civitas* capitals and the irregular layout of streets in minor settlements, which developed at particular points along the road system for reasons other than administrative necessity, could not be more marked (compare Figs.1 and 2).

Nor can it be argued that this reflects nothing more than the superior wealth and development of the larger settlements. The walled town of Chesterton (Durobrivae) was considerably larger and apparently more developed than the *civitas* capital of Caistor by Norwich (Venta Icenorum). Yet Chesterton displays an *ad hoc* development of side-streets leading off the main road through the town (Fig.2). By contrast, at Caistor the dominance of an imposed grid pattern is evident, despite certain irregularities. If, as might be suggested, the formal street pattern at Caistor is simply a local attempt to emulate Roman town planning, why, it must be asked, was this supposed emulation confined to those settlements which had been selected as administrative centres ?

At the same time, it is interesting to note that the street grid in *civitas* capitals is not always primary as it is in colonies founded on previously unoccupied sites. At Silchester, for example, there are a number of buildings which appear to follow an alignment other than that of the street system. These, it has been suggested, reflect the early development of the town, presumably prior to the establishment of its formal status as capital of the

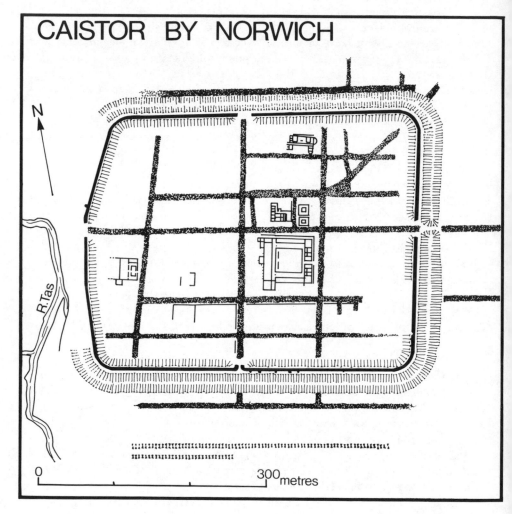

Fig. 1. Plan of the *civitas* at Caistor by Norwich (*Venta Icenorum*), showing the original street-grid extending beyond the town walls.

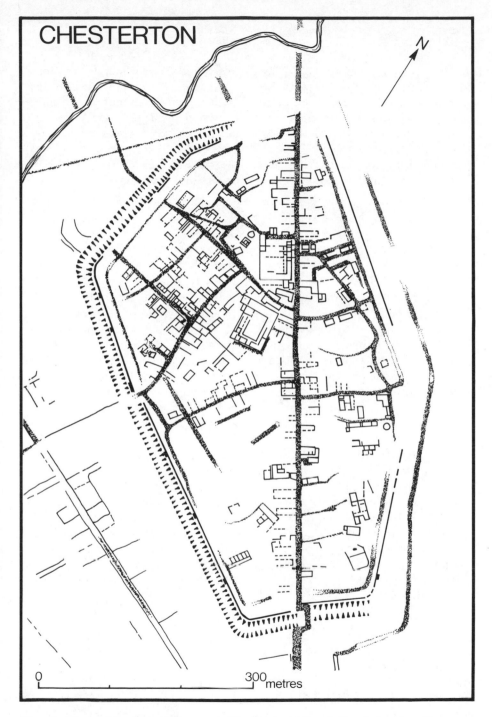

Fig. 2. Plan of the 'small' town at Chesterton (*Durobrivae*) showing the
ad hoc development of the street-system.

Atrebates (Boon 1974, 47). Though these buildings, which are of stone
construction, are themselves unlikely to date from the establishment of the
town, they may be reconstructions of earlier timber buildings on the same
alignment. Similarly in Gaul, the early development of urban settlement
forms prior to their establishment as administrative centres may have resulted in the street grid being inserted later (Drinkwater 1985, 52-3). The
upheaval involved surely implies control by some single overriding authority; the most likely candidate is the Roman administration.

   More direct assistance to town building may have been provided. There
is evidence which has been taken to indicate direct military involvement
in urban planning. For example, the similarity in plan between the *fora*
in British towns and military headquarters buildings has been considered
significant, though some doubt has recently been cast on its implications
(Blagg 1984). That the plan of one of the early buildings at Verulamium is
reminiscent of a barrack block is only slightly more convincing (Frere 1972,
10-11), though the building method employed, a quite sophisticated form
of sleeper-beam construction, is not easily paralleled in the late pre-Roman
Iron Age in south-east Britain. It is, however, well attested in first century
Roman military contexts, though such similarities might simply reflect the
influence of the military as models for native work. The extent to which
military assistance was provided for civilian building projects is a matter
of debate. The various literary references and inscriptions which provide
evidence of this process are not as common as has been implied: a number
of the latter which have been cited actually refer to purely military works
(*pace* Macmullen 1959, 214-22). Even those inscriptions which do record
construction for apparently non-military purposes tend to be concerned
with more general matters such as the provincial infrastructure (roads and
aqueducts), the propitiation of the gods (temples) or the provision of leisure
facilities (baths and amphitheatres). Moreover, they relate in the main to
colonies with populations made up largely of army veterans (Fentress 1979,
161-71). Explicit references are rare. In Egypt, under Probus, soldiers seem
to have been responsible for various forms of building work and engineering
in town and country alike, if we can trust the account of the *Historia
Augusta*:

> The works which he made his soldiers carry out can still be
> seen in many cities in Egypt. He did so much on the Nile
> that his efforts alone added greatly to the amount of grain
> brought in as tribute. He had bridges, temples, colonnades
> and public buildings erected by army labour. Many river
> mouths were opened up. Many marshes were drained and
> replaced by grain-fields and farms. (SHA *Probus* 9.3).

We may reasonably conclude that town construction was at least encouraged by the Roman authorities, for such foundations provided the simplest
way of centralising the administration of newly acquired territory. But
despite official encouragement, the history of urban development suggests
that some towns were slow to get off the ground or failed to live up to
expectations. It has been noted in Britain, for example, that the earliest
non-public buildings in *civitas* capitals tend to be so-called 'strip buildings',
fairly modest structures which often combine the function of house, shop
and workshop. More elaborate houses, the residences of the wealthy elite,
do not appear in towns until the mid-second century AD, though their
rural counterparts, the villas, began to appear shortly after the conquest
(Walthew 1975). Thus it would appear that it was some time before the
ruling elite, on whom Roman local administrative organisation depended,
were willing to live in these new towns. The relationship between the town
walls and the street grid at Caistor by Norwich in Britain is also instruc-
tive. Here the pattern of streets extends beyond the enclosed area, which
suggests that the extent of the town as originally envisaged had not been
attained by the time that the defences were erected (Fig.1). While at other
towns, such as Autun and Amiens in Gaul, we see quite large areas within
the walls which were apparently never built upon (Drinkwater 1983, 144).
The reasons for these phenomena are quite uncertain, but they are probably a reflection of the different reactions to Roman occupation of different
tribal groups, or simply local variations in economic development.

In some parts of the empire, however, towns were either very slow to appear
or failed to appear at all. How were these areas administered?

Since military occupation was usually the first stage in the control of
most newly acquired territory, it is not surprising to find evidence that the
administration remained in the hands of the army. There is clear epigraphic
evidence from several provinces of a legionary centurion or local auxiliary
unit commander with responsibility for direct administrative supervision
of an otherwise tribal organisation, usually with the title *praefectus civi-
tatis*. In Moesia under Augustus or Tiberius a senior centurion of *legio* V
Macedonica was acting as *praefectus civitatium* of two tribes, the Moesi
and the Trebelli (*CIL* 5.1838). Similarly, in Dalmatia under Nero or Vespasian a centurion of *legio* XI Claudia was *praefectus civitatium* of both
the Maezaei and Daesitiates (*CIL* 9. 2564). In Pannonia under Claudius
a senior centurion of *legio* XIII Gemina was entrusted with the *praefectura*
of the *civitas Colapianorum* (*CIL* 3.14387), while in the same province un-

der the Flavians the commander of *cohors I Noricorum* was simultaneously *praefectus ripae Danuvii et civitatium duarum Boiorum et Azaliorum* (*CIL* 9.5363). Though no such offices are attested in Gaul or Britain, it seems reasonable to suppose, as already suggested, that administrative responsibility would have rested in military hands until it was formally handed over to civil authorities which were eventually established in the *civitas* capitals (Rivet 1977, 169; Wightman 1977, 122-3). The absence of direct evidence in these areas may be explained by the fact that it was only a temporary expedient there, whereas in Dalmatia, Pannonia and Moesia the system remained in use for a number of years (Mocsy 1974, 134-5). It is possible, however, that the third century inscriptions from Ribchester in northern England, which refer to a legionary centurion as *praepositus numeri et regionis* (*RIB* 583 and 587), may represent fundamentally the same system in operation. More recently it has been noted that among the writing-tablets recovered from Vindolanda is a letter which refers to a *centurio regionarius* based at Carlisle probably in the reign of Trajan (Bowman and Thomas 1983, 110), while an undated altar from Bath was dedicated by a *centurio regionarius* (*RIB* 152). Though the precise function of such an office is uncertain, the title might imply that its holder's authority extended beyond the purely military sphere. Indeed, we find a centurion *regendis Frisiis impositus* levying taxes in AD 28:

> Drusus had imposed on them a moderate tribute commensurate with their limited resources - a payment of ox- hides for military purposes. No-one paid particular attention to their durability or size until Olennius, a senior centurion appointed to govern the Frisii, chose auroch-hides (i.e. large hides) as the standard for contributions. That demand, harsh in any context, was all the more difficult for the Germans to bear, for, though their land contains large creatures in the wild, their domestic herds are of moderate size. (Tac.*Ann*.4.72).

As an alternative to military control if the native population did not require a garrison, or as a later development when Roman confidence in the security of an area grew, some *civitates* became autonomous territories under the control of a *praefectus* or *praepositus* appointed from among the local aristocracy (*principes*). Once again the evidence is epigraphic and comes from the central European provinces. Among a series of dedications to Neptune by *principes* of the Iapodes in Dalmatia are three with the title *praepositus* and one, who also possesses Roman citizenship, with the title *praefectus* (*CIL* 3.14324-8). Similarly from Pannonia comes a *princeps praefectus* of the Scordisci, who obtained his Roman citizenship from the Flavian dynasty (Mocsy 1957). The principle of employing the indigenous aristocracy to control annexed areas is not unlike that of Rome's relationship with native kings. Indeed, Julius Cottius, the son of one such monarch, is recorded on the inscription on an arch at Susa as *praefectus* of fourteen named *civitates* in the Cottian Alps (*CIL* 5.7231)—Cottius' own son was subsequently restored as king.

Certain principles begin to emerge within these local variations in Roman practice. Firstly, that as far as possible administrative control was left in the hands of the local population. The central government employed very few administrators within the provinces. It has been calculated that in the middle of the second century AD there was one elite official for every 300,000 provincials. That ratio contrasts sharply with the figures produced for China in the twelfth century AD, where there was one gentry official for every 15,000 people (Hopkins 1983, 186). In the absence of a large professional civil service, central government relied heavily on local notables to supervise tax-collection, to maintain roads and services and to keep order in their locality. Secondly, Roman authorities dealt exclusively with local elites. Even in remote areas such as Scotland where there are few literary or epigraphic references, the archaeological evidence seems to confirm this. During the brief periods of occupation in the first and second centuries AD, Roman goods find their way on to a very limited number of native sites. These tend to be the unusual, exotic or larger sites such as lowland brochs, souterrain settlements or larger hillforts such as Traprain Law, the homes of the native aristocracy (Macinnes 1984 and 1988). The goods do not filter far down the social hierarchy, and coinage hardly at all. Thus contact with Rome, exemplified by artefacts either traded or presented as diplomatic gifts, was restricted to the upper echelons of native society who used their control of these new and desirable imports to support their own position within that social order.

Having established that the Romans both desired and encouraged urbanisation in areas which they annexed, the question arises why in certain areas did it take so long or even fail to materialise altogether. The answer lies not with the Romans, but with the peoples that they conquered. If we look at the areas where urbanisation progressed with fair rapidity, we find that at the time of the Roman conquest they were already well advanced towards developed centralised settlement forms. They might be termed proto-urban, with many of the functions that we associate with urban life. Thus even before the arrival of the Romans in central Gaul, for example, we find large settlements, usually referred to as *oppida*, such as Bibracte (Mont Beuvray), located in excellent defensive positions. Their inhabitants are not exclusively occupied in agriculture, for there is widespread evidence of craft specialisation and wealth distinction. The sites are also characterised by a relative abundance of Roman imports, particularly items concerned with feasting, especially drinking, and by quantities of Gallic bronze coinage (Nash 1976). Looking further afield, such late La Tène *oppida* are found widely distributed across western and central Europe, bounded in the north by the southern edge of the north European Plain (Collis 1984, 8-14). South-eastern England may also be included within this distribution map of areas of proto-urban settlement, albeit as a late developer. Although archaeological investigation of these sites in England has been relatively limited, they are readily recognised by their large size. Moreover, they display associations similar to those of their Gallic counterparts: they were operating in an economic system based on coinage and there is no shortage of evidence of trade with Rome, particularly wine-amphorae (Cunliffe 1976, 142-56). It is perhaps no coincidence that the limits of proto-urban development in Europe prior to the Roman occupation correspond broadly with what became the northern frontier of the Roman empire (Fig.3).

Nor can this be explained simply as the ability of certain areas to support concentrations of population - an explanation akin to geographical determinism. For in large parts of eastern Europe which lie beyond the Roman empire and beyond the spread of pre-Roman *oppida*, urban sites became well established by the eleventh century AD. This was a direct result of social and political development, namely the rise of the mediaeval nation state (Dejevsky 1980).

It seems reasonable to suggest, therefore, that the speed of development of Romanised towns in conquered provinces was a direct reflection of the extent to which the local people had already begun to develop urban forms of settlement, which carries with it the implication that they had also established an appropriate economic infrastructure (Groenman van Waateringe 1980). Also of importance was the extent of previous contact with the Mediterranean world. If the local aristocracy had already obtained a taste for the trappings of Roman civilisation, it would be that much easier for them to see the possible benefits of Roman rule after any initial resistance to the conquest and the loss of their independence. Indeed, in some cases, such as in Noricum, prior contact of this nature made military conquest unnecessary. Outside the walls of Magdalensberg, the largest *oppidum* in the region and the seat of the Norican kings, we see the establishment of a Roman trading settlement by 100 BC. Continued close trading relations and the presence of Roman merchants contributed to the Romanisation of the native inhabitants as well as to their wealth, and ensured good political relations between Rome and the Norican kings. When the Romans finally occupied the country in 15 BC no force was necessary and the Magdalensberg became the centre of Roman administration for the province (Alfoldy

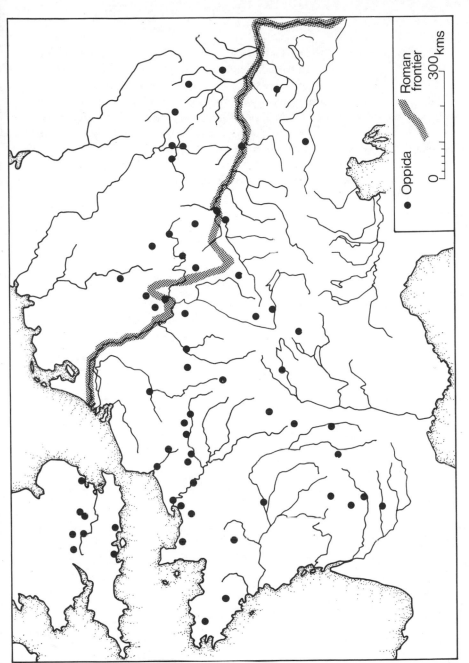

Fig. 3. The European frontier of the Roman empire in the second century AD plotted against the distribution of pre-Roman, proto-urban settlements (*oppida*).

1974, 40-47).

The importance of the attitude of the new provincial population cannot be overstressed. The continued success and expansion of the Roman empire was as much a consequence of this process of assimilation as it was of the prowess of the army. In simple physical terms, the Roman empire could not have grown far if it had been necessary to station troops every few miles in order to control the local population. Stability and further expansion depended upon the processes of assimilation and acculturation: the acceptance, adoption, and perhaps adaptation, of Roman civilisation and its values. Good government and effective administration require co-operation.

Client Kings

DAVID C. BRAUND

As Rome expanded through the Mediterranean world and beyond she encountered states and communities of many types—a large number of these
were monarchies of various sorts. At every stage in the history of Roman
expansion a significant proportion of the Roman sphere was under the administration of monarchs. Modern scholars regularly refer to such kings
as 'client kings'. The term is convenient and familiar, but, as will become
apparent, it is at best very imprecise. The term 'client kings' has also come
to carry with it a range of misconceptions, of which the most important
demand immediate attention.

1. *Annexation* (so-called: see Introduction). Contrary to familiar notions,
there is no evidence that Romans thought of these monarchs as temporary stop-gaps, to be replaced one day by provincial administrations—
indeed, such long-term planning is not characteristic of Roman government. It is true that by the end of the first century AD the most familiar
client kingdoms—Galatia, Cappadocia, Commagene etc.—had ceased to
be monarchies and were governed instead by a Roman official. But there
had been no great move away from the use of client kings in general. And
certain areas—for example, the Crimea, Armenia and much of northern Europe, especially beyond the Rhine and Danube—remained, into the Later
Roman Empire, the preserves of various monarchs who may be considered

client kings. Throughout Roman history into the Middle Ages client kings continued to perform vital roles in the Roman world.

Annexations had taken place in a piecemeal fashion, encouraged by essentially local factors. A royal family might fall under suspicion of treachery against Rome, as, we are told, did that of Commagene in AD 72 (Jos.*BJ* 7.219ff.). A more widespread and recurrent problem was the instability of monarchies in periods of succession. Where there was no obvious successor, disorder and local civil warfare threatened to break out—a powerful incitement for Rome to annex (see, in general, Goody 1966). In particular, local elites might well prefer direct Roman rule (with all the freedom of action that that might entail) to the rule of a monarch whom they feared. The aftermath of Herod's death shows these factors at work (e.g.Jos.*BJ* 2.91). The worst excesses of Roman provincial government should not lead us to imagine that local elites were inevitably, or even commonly, opposed to annexation by Rome. Much depended on the available alternative (cf. Bernhardt 1985 on the attitudes of cities). Nor should it be supposed automatically that Rome was eager to annex: in fact, for the Republican period in particular, scholars are still striving fully to understand why Rome was so notably reluctant to create new territorial provinces.

Annexations of client kingdoms are best understood not as a masterstroke of some grand imperial strategy, but as a series of Roman responses to particular and localised royal failures. That is not to say, of course, that piecemeal, reactive annexations could not be incorporated within broader, more considered changes: the annexation of Commagene in AD 72 was part of a broader re-structuring of the eastern frontier, though the evidence indicates that it was also a reaction to a particular situation—the Roman response was judicious (cf.Kennedy 1984). More generally, annexations could satisfy local demands in some cases and give further scope for the aggrandizement of imperial prestige and, possibly, wealth. It is also probably reasonable to imagine, with the majority of scholars, that contact with Rome over centuries made local elites, in particular, more ripe and perhaps more eager for annexation. However, it is also reasonable to doubt that Rome planned such assimilation with a view to annexation in the long term. In the case of client kingdoms, acculturation to Rome was in essence a by-product of Roman concern to exercise broad control and of the eagerness of at least some local rulers and elites to participate in Roman society and share in Roman power. In so far as Romans did encourage Romanisation (see the other articles in this volume), they did so to promote order, to facilitate administration and, perhaps, to advance and extend Roman cultural traditions after or in the process of annexation.

2. *Variations among kings.* The monarchs of the Roman world varied greatly from one to another. They differed widely in their local traditions— for example, they included rulers of Jewish kingdoms, the Ptolemies, the tribal chieftains who proliferated especially in the West and many more besides. Some rulers were women, as Tacitus observes in the case of Britain (Tac.*Agr.*16); a woman—under the name or title 'Candace' —also ruled at times over Meroe, situated to the south of Egypt (Strabo 18 p.820; Plin.*NH* 6.29 and 186; cf.*Acts* 8.27; Dio 54.5). And queens could wield great power, as did the famous Cleopatra VII of Egypt or Dynamis of the Bosporan Kingdom in the Crimea and Pythodoris of Pontus early in the first century AD (see, for example, Macurdy 1937). Moreover, the nature of the ruler's authority varied from kingdom to kingdom: Tacitus, again, observes the rather unkingly nature of the monarch's position in certain tribal societies (Tac.*Ann.*13.54.2).

The physical geography and positions of kingdoms were also immensely varied, of course. Some client kings ruled mountainous territories, like those of the Antilebanon, the Taurus Mountains, the Caucasus and the so-called 'Celtic fringe' of Britain. Some ruled over forests and marshes, others over great plains and deserts. Some ruled land-locked kingdoms, others ruled on coasts. The majority ruled on the margins of Roman power and influence, but a few ruled kingdoms surrounded by provinces. A case in point is the kingdom of Cogidubnus in S.E. Britain in the region of Sussex. Cogidubnus' kingdom was not on the margins of the Roman empire, except perhaps in the earliest stages of Claudius' invasion of Britain in AD 43. Cogidubnus has been compared to Cottius II, his contemporary, who ruled in the Maritime Alps, sandwiched between N.W. Italy and S.E. Gaul— both areas which had been under direct Roman rule for very many years (Bogaers 1979; Barrett 1979). Other cases are less clear-cut. For example, the Thracian kingdom was in one sense evidently not on the margin of the empire after the creation of the province of Moesia between it and the Danube under Augustus; the kingdom continued until AD 46. Yet there was also a sense in which it was marginal to the Roman empire, for it included refractory hill-dwellers, who defied control by the Thracian kings, let alone Rome (Tac.*Ann.*6.42). It is seldom sufficiently understood that provinces and kingdoms were not neatly separated, for example, into concentric circles with provinces on the inside and kingdoms on the outside. The province of Syria was peppered with principalities (see Millar 1987 and the literature there cited on the cultural and political complexity of the area). The kingdom of Mauretania, from 25 BC to AD 40, contained within its territory some Roman colonies, which were under the jurisdiction not of the king of Mauretania but of the Roman governor of Baetica in southern Spain, across the Straits of Gibraltar (Plin.*NH* 5.2 with Braund 1984 101n.48 and Mackie 1983b).

And of course kingdoms varied according to their power, both economically and militarily. Each ruler ruled in his own particular context. All these variations could not but be significant in the relationship between a particular ruler on the one hand and the Roman state and individual Romans on the other. Indeed, some kings were so powerful that, though comparable to client kings in many respects, they are seldom considered (by modern scholars and most ancient sources alike) to have been client kings at all. The outstanding case must be Parthia, whence, for example, princes were in several instances sent to Rome for their 'education' under the Julio-Claudians, like the sons of client kings such as the Herods (Tac.*Ann.*12.10-11 is tantalising; cf.Braund 1984, 9-21). Among other powerful kings who resemble client kings in varying degree, may be mentioned Antiochus III of Syria after the Treaty of Apamea (188/7 BC) and Mithridates VI of Pontus and Decebalus of Dacia when they were not actually at war with Rome.

And of course there were significant changes over time. In the mid-second century BC, when Attalus II of Pergamum and his court discussed their military plans, the importance of Rome was accepted, but only after protracted discussion. The proceedings are recorded in outline in a letter of Attalus II to Attis, priest of Cybele at Pessinus, which survives in the form of an inscription:

> ...When we came to Pergamum and I assembled Athenaeus, Sosander and Menogenes and many others of my 'relatives', and when I laid before them what we discussed in Apamea and told them our decision, there was a very long discussion. At first everyone tended to agree with us, but Chlorus vehemently drew our attention to Roman power and advised us to do nothing at all without the Romans. Few agreed with him at first, but subsequently, as we pondered the matter day after day, Chlorus' view became more and more attractive: it became apparent that to start something without the Romans involved considerable danger. For in the event of success we would become the objects of envy, detraction and very damaging suspicion—which the Romans felt towards my brother—while failure would be simple disaster. For the Romans would be pleased, not sympathetic, at our plight, because we had set about something of this nature without them. But, as it is, if—perish the thought—we were to suffer any setbacks, we would receive help and could recover our losses (with the good-will of the gods) because we have acted with the full knowledge of the Romans and according to their advice. I decided, therefore, to send to Rome at every stage

> men to make constant reports of what is at issue, while [we]
> ourselves make [thorough] preparation [so that if it is neces-
> sary] we may help ourselves... (Welles 1934, no.61).

Within decades such discussions became unnecessary: the importance of
Rome in Asia Minor was immediately obvious once Rome had established
the province of Asia upon the death of Attalus III, had fought major wars
with Mithridates VI of Pontus and had annexed the kingdom of Bithynia.

3. *Variations at Rome.* The social and political situation at Rome also
changed greatly over time as traditional competition and conflict became
civil war and the Republic became the Principate. Patronage was fundamental to Roman society: a major aspect of peer-group rivalry in that
society was competition for clients, particularly clients of high status for
they conferred special prestige upon their patrons. Kings had high status.
Sometimes Romans might seek to elevate their own status by demeaning
kings, as perhaps did Popilius Laenas when he demanded an answer on the
spot from Antiochus IV in 168 BC (protecting Ptolemaic Egypt, it should
be noted: Polybius 29.26-7). Similarly Romans might seek to exploit their
conquest of kings by, for example, parading them in triumphal processions
through Rome.

For all that, there was a strong feeling at Rome that kings were especially exalted beings. Indeed, their prominence in triumphs tends to
indicate as much. And kings were expected to behave with a kingly dignity appropriate to their status. King Prusias II of Bithynia was decried
for grovelling in the Senate (Polybius 30.18; Livy 45.44). By contrast, a
captured king who exhibited the haughty spirit which the Romans deemed
proper for a king, might be treated with a certain respect: the attitude of
Mithridates VIII, king of the Crimean Bosporus, became something of a
legend:

> It was said that he talked with the emperor (Claudius) in a
> manner more fierce than his misfortune suggested. One of
> his statements, in these words, gained wide currency: 'I have
> not been sent to you—I have come to you. If you doubt it,
> send me away and find me'. His appearance, likewise, never
> showed a sign of fear, even when he was put on show by the
> rostra, surrounded by guards, as a spectacle for the people.
> (Tac.*Ann.*12.21).

Mithridates lived on at Rome until executed by Galba for complicity in
Nymphidius Sabinus' imperial ambitions in AD 68 (Plut.*Galba* 13-15). Of
course, defeated kings could be and were executed, whether haughty or not.

But the view remained strong at Rome, nevertheless, that a king should conduct himself in a kingly manner and that his status should be accorded the appropriate privileges (cf.Rawson 1975). If the king were to be chained, then gold or silver chains might be used. Thus, when Antony paraded Artavasdes, king of Armenia, in chains, he used gold chains, we are told, 'lest his [i.e. the king's] status be at all diminished' (*ne quid honori deesset*: Vell.Pat. 2.82—the later Dio 49.39 says they were silver chains). Octavian too is said to have paraded kings in golden chains at Rome (Prop.2.1.33). In the third century AD the emperor Aurelian is said to have held a triumph in which he paraded Zenobia in chains of gold (SHA *Tyr. Trig.* 30.26; *Aur.* 34.3). After the triumph Aurelian gave her a villa at Tibur (Tivoli) where she lived out her days, we are told, as a Roman *matrona* (SHA *Tyr. Trig.*30.27; Eutrop.9.13.2). It is possible that she left descendants there (Baldini 1978). When royalty were detained, their conditions of detention, it was argued, should be appropriate to their high status. Thus, in the mid-second century BC, L. Aemilius Paullus had the captive King Perseus of Macedon housed in comfortable surroundings after a brief and demeaning period in less congenial conditions (Plut.*Aem.* 37). It seems that in most cases (though there are exceptions) a detained king could expect to be housed in style. We should therefore take seriously the tradition that Octavian offered Cleopatra a comfortable existence should she surrender and allow herself to be paraded in triumph. Whether Octavian's offer is historical or not, it is entirely concordant with Roman practice. Cleopatra preferred suicide and was therefore thought worthy of admiration for so keen a concern for the proprieties of her royal status (Horace, *Odes* 1.37). By contrast, Maroboduus preferred a quiet existence at Ravenna as a diplomatic tool of Tiberius and thus, in Tacitus' view, 'grew old with a reputation greatly diminished by his excessive desire to live on' (*Ann.*2.63): he should, it is implied, have died like Cleopatra.

That Romans might recognise royal status and treat royalty with special respect should not altogether surprise. A fundamental characteristic of Roman legal thought and action was inequality before the law: those of high status could expect markedly better treatment and less punishment than those of low status (Garnsey 1970). At the same time it was also held that fortune could bring down any great individual, including important Romans, such as provincial governors: Cicero urges upon his brother the view that, exceptionally, the province of Asia offers little scope for the malign effects of fortune upon a governor (Cic.*ad Q.fr.*1.1). Throughout antiquity, a favourite example of ill-fortune at work was the reduction of a king to slavery (e.g.Juvenal 7.201 and, in general, Nussbaum 1986). The *Ad Herennium*, a late Republican rhetorical treatise ascribed to Cicero, tells us not only that such a fall evoked pity (2.50) but also that for a victor to treat a defeated king well was to the victor's credit, a mark of his *humanitas* against the common enemy, fortune (*Ad Her.* 2.80: 4.23 cf. Sen. *De Clem.* 1.1). As Tacitus' Caratacus told Claudius: 'if you save my life, I shall be an everlasting memorial of your clemency' (*Ann.* 12.37).

The *Res Gestae* boasts not only that Augustus was a conqueror of kings but also that kings had come to seek his friendship and his protection, in some cases over great distances, including potentially hostile kings. Under the Republic there had been competition for royal clients: when Eumenes II of Pergamum came to Rome on the eve of the Third Macedonian War, leading Romans vied to be near him (Plut. *Cato Maior* 8, where Cato's hostility to kings, though familiar enough, is evidently meant to be unusual). In the late Republic Cicero strove to have visiting royalty lodge with him, while all the time complaining that others were striving to do the same (*ad Att.*13.2a). Under the Principate the emperor needed to excel in areas wherein the elite had competed under the Republic—thus, he must excel in having kings as clients. Hence, the claims for Augustus in the *Res Gestae*. Yet, ideally, the excellence of the *princeps* should not exclude the Roman elite at large: Tacitus complains that under the Principate it is no longer possible, as it was under the Republic, 'to cultivate and be cultivated by kings' (*Ann.* 3.55). Part of the problem for Tacitus and other senators like him will have been that kings understood the realities of power and authority at Rome and will themselves have concentrated their attentions upon the emperor and those most closely associated with him.

Prestige is very much at issue. But it was by no means only on account of prestige that the emperor tended to monopolise personal relationships with kings. Kings controlled vast resources of men, materials and wealth. The great hellenistic kingdoms, notably Seleucid Syria, Ptolemaic Egypt and Attalid Pergamum, remained a force to be reckoned with even at their nadir. The resources and manpower of Cleopatra's Egypt were a mainstay of Antony's position in the East. Less well-known rulers also had great power at their disposal. When Cicero was governor in Cilicia in 51/0 BC, Deiotarus of Galatia possessed two legions—his own men trained and equipped in the Roman fashion (Cic.*ad Att.* 6.1.14; *Bell.Alex.* 34.4). Juba I of Numidia is said to have fielded his own four legions in 46 BC (*Bell.Afr.* 1 with Brunt 1971, 474). Under the Principate, military strength and resources of this order would be critical in the event of revolt against the emperor and civil warfare. Particularly clear is the case of Vespasian: Tacitus indicates the contribution made to his cause by client kings in the East:

> Additions to his cause, with their kingdoms, were Sohaemus, whose strength was not to be despised, and Antiochus, who had enormous ancestral wealth and was the richest of the kings who serve Rome. Before long Agrippa [II] was called back from the city of Rome by his friends' secret messengers; while Vitellius was still in ignorance, Agrippa had rushed off in a swift ship. Queen Berenice was no less zealous in her support for Vespasian. She was at her peak in age and beauty and was attractive to old Vespasian, too, through the splendour of her gifts...[and in the subsequent gathering of the principals at Berytus]...the show made by so much cavalry and infantry and by so many kings vying with each other was a spectacle befitting the fortune of an emperor. (Tac.*Hist.*2.81).

King Sohaemus of Emesa and King Antiochus of Commagene, together with the Jewish royals, King Agrippa (II) and his sister Queen Berenice, clearly made substantial contributions to Vespasian's cause in material terms. At the same time they made him look the part—such a royal cavalcade gave him the air of imperial greatness on Tacitus' interpretation.

It was probably his appreciation of the kings' potential for revolt as well, no doubt, as his concern for his prestige, that led Claudius to degrade a Roman governor for being 'a companion of a king in his province' (Suet.*Claud.* 16.2; cf.*Nero* 37.1). It has been suggested that the emperor Gaius had King Ptolemy of Mauretania killed in AD 40 on the grounds that the king was involved in a broader conspiracy against him, with Gaetulicus at its head (Fishwick and Shaw 1976). According to Josephus a principal charge against Herod Antipas was that he had conspired first with Sejanus against the emperor Tiberius and thereafter with the Parthian king against the emperor Gaius. In consequence Gaius removed Antipas from power and exiled him to the West, probably to Lyons (Jos.*AJ* 18.250). We have noted, above, the execution of Mithridates VIII for his support of Nymphidius Sabinus, the praetorian prefect who wished to be emperor in AD 68.

It should by now be evident that the change from Republic to Principate brought a marked change in the relationships between kings, Rome and Romans. As we shall see, the period of civil warfare which generated the Principate was the period of greatest innovation in these relationships: Antony seems to have been responsible for much of that innovation. These changes were so marked and so significant that Suetonius notices and draws attention to them:

> As to the kingdoms which he gained by right of conquest, he either returned them to those from whom he had taken them or joined them to unrelated kingdoms, with a few exceptions. He also linked the allied kings with one another by establishing connections between them: he was very ready to suggest or support their marriage-alliances and friendships. He took care of them all as if they were limbs and organs of empire. It was also his custom to appoint a man to guide those young in years or unstable in mind, until they became adults or recovered. He brought up and educated the children of many kings together with his own family. (Suet.*Aug.*48).

and:

> The friendly and allied kings each founded cities called Caesarea in their own kingdoms. And they all decided together to complete at their joint expense the temple of Olympian Jupiter at Athens, begun long ago, and to dedicate it to the Genius of Augustus. And they often left their kingdoms to pay their daily respects to him in the manner of clients, wearing togas and without their royal insignia. This they did not only at Rome, but also as he was travelling about the provinces. (Suet.*Aug.*60).

Kings displayed evident respect for Augustus. They left aside the paraphernalia that expressed their regal status and marked them out as kings. But they did not grovel and behave as freedmen, like the despised Prusias. They were dignified. They wore the toga, the particular symbol of Roman citizenship and with that, more broadly, peaceful participation in the Roman sphere—note the Celtiberians of Spain, who were 'called togati, as being peaceful and having changed to gentleness and Italian ways, dressed in their togas' (Strabo 3. p.167). Augustus was like the kings' patron, watching over their affairs and lending a helping hand when needed: as Suetonius puts it, 'he took care of them all' (*Aug.*48). Suetonius' analysis and the situation he describes must be understood as one facet of the broad idea that the Roman empire was beneficial and protective towards its subjects, an idea common to Republic and Principate alike (Brunt 1978). Under the Principate, the emperor, who claimed to be the leading man and greatest benefactor in the Roman state, took the work of imperial beneficence upon himself.

Ancient sources repeatedly and quite consistently fail to use the term 'client' of a king in relation to Rome. Moreover, it is most unusual to find a king described as the client of an individual Roman, though this occasionally happens (see Braund 1984, 29-30; Rich 1988 is valuable on the whole issue). The Romans called these kings 'friends and allies', as does Suetonius in the passage quoted above. It should be noted that Suetonius describes their behaviour even towards Augustus as being 'in the manner of clients' (*more clientium: Aug*.48). They are not so much clients as like clients. The terminological debate swiftly becomes sterile, yet one aspect of that debate deserves particular attention here. It is easy to forget that it is not just kings but the whole of the empire that was conceived as being under the beneficent protection of Rome. And 'friends and allies' of the Roman state are to be found elsewhere in the empire. Indeed, the term 'allies' (*socii*) is regularly applied by our sources to those whom we now describe as 'provincials' (Sherwin-White 1973, 188). And there were whole cities whose populations could be described as the clients of a particular Roman and his family (e.g.Cic.*De Rep*.1.43; cf.Reynolds in this volume on patronage-agreements). Individual provincials, too, might be not only *clientes* and *amici* of particular Romans and Roman families, but also, like kings, 'friends and allies' of the Roman state (Bernhardt 1985, 133). In short, any notion of kings with some special 'client' status in the Roman empire is nonsense. And it is a particularly dangerous nonsense because it obscures just how much so-called client kings had in common with the rest of the empire. Crawford is right to assert that 'the Romans possessed no juridical concept of a client state' (Crawford 1985, 268). However, the term 'client king' is unlikely to be dislodged and must therefore be tolerated.

Suetonius indicates that there was a religious aspect to the relationship between Augustus and the kings, as there was to the relationship between the emperor and the empire at large (Price 1984). Under the Republic we hear nothing of royal involvement in the provincial cults of individual Romans or in the cult of Roma. We find, rather, that kings made dedications to Jupiter on the Capitol at Rome and honoured Capitoline Jupiter in their kingdoms in a few cases (Braund 1984, 113). It should be noted that civic communities of the empire shared their concern for the Capitol and Jupiter: surviving inscriptions include both royal and civic dedications (Lintott 1978). After the battle of Pydna in 168 BC Massinissa, king of Numidia, wished to offer sacrifice on the Capitol (Livy 45.13- 14). The Capitol was a focal point of the Roman state—Livy calls it 'the citadel of empire..., the head of things' (1.55). Cicero describes a dedication in the temple of Capitoline Jupiter as 'a monument of alliance and friendship for the Roman people, in the most famous of temples' (*In Verr.* 2.4.67). Josephus tells us how a senatorial procession, with Herod to the fore, paraded up to the Capitol in 40 BC: there they sacrificed and deposited the treaty by which Herod had just been formally recognised (Jos.*AJ* 14.379-89;

cf.Cic.*Rab.Post*.6).

The Capitol retained great significance under the Principate. Under Augustus British rulers made sacrifices there (Strabo 4.p.200). Under Antoninus Pius, King Pharasmanes of Iberia (in the Caucasus) sacrificed there (Dio 69.15.3). The imperial cult did not replace royal concern for Jupiter and the Capitol. The imperial cult was something new in the relationships between kings and Rome and Romans. It was a further expression of the greater coherence achieved by Augustus with regard to the kings and the empire in general.

In the Bosporan kingdom on the north shore of the Black Sea the local rulers repeatedly proclaimed themselves the high priests of the imperial cult. The Bosporan case is exceptional, but only in degree. The *urbes Caesareae* established by kings, like Herod, Juba II of Mauretania and others, were focal points of the imperial cult. Josephus describes how, for example, Herod's Caesarea (previously the Greek city of Strato's Tower), which he made a key harbour-city of the eastern Mediterranean, was dominated by an imposing temple of Rome and Augustus:

> In a circle round the harbour lay a ring of buildings bedecked with the most polished stone. In the centre of that ring there was a hill on which stood a temple of the emperor, in full view of sailors as they sailed into the harbour: the temple contained two statues—one of Rome and one of the emperor. (Jos.*AJ* 15.339).

The foundation (or re-foundation) of such cities was celebrated by festivals redolent of imperial cult and supported by the imperial family. The very name Caesarea ('Caesar-city') proclaimed the imperial connection. Moreover, these cities and others in the kingdoms contained monuments, buildings and even rooms named after members of the imperial family. Antony, it seems, was the first Roman to be honoured in this way by kings: we find a city in Paphlagonia called Antoniopolis (cf.Braund 1984, 118n.38) and in Jerusalem Herod named the Antonia fortress after Antony (Jos.*AJ* 15.409).

Royal dynasties might also include, among their family names, the names of members of the imperial family. King Agrippa I of Judaea seems to have been named after M.Vipsanius Agrippa. Two of Agrippa I's daughters bore traditional family names (Mariamme, Berenice), while another daughter (Drusilla) and his two sons (Agrippa, Drusus) had Roman names: Drusilla was probably named after the sister of the emperor Gaius, while Drusus may well have been named after Tiberius' son (and Agrippa I's friend) of that name (Braund 1984, 111; cf.47n.8 for names such as Italicus, which are found especially among rulers of the West). Kings had not taken Roman names under the Republic.

As part of their titulature kings proclaimed themselves 'friend of Rome' and 'friend of Caesar'. Sometimes they named a particular emperor, as did Herod of Chalcis when he called himself friend of Claudius on coins he issued in AD 43 (Smallwood 1967, no.210). Similarly, cities might be named not only Caesarea or Sebaste (the Greek version of Augusta), but also Tiberias, Neronias and the like (e.g.Smallwood 1967, no.211). Under the Republic we find kings described only as *philorhomaeus*, 'friend of Rome', and that not before the first century BC: their titulature does not link them to any particular Roman—no king, for example, called himself *philopompeius*, 'friend of Pompey'. In this matter, as in so much else, the change seems to have come with Antony, when Tarcondimotus of Cilicia used the epithet *philantonius*, 'friend of Antony' (Braund 1984, 105).

Royal coinage commonly bore imperial heads, though there is no real evidence that emperors were concerned to control or limit royal rights of coinage. Under the Republic Roman heads had not appeared on royal coinage. Crawford's interpretation of the change deserves quotation:

> The most dramatic expression...on the coinage of the Roman world of the unity of that world under Augustus is the flood of issues bearing his portrait ; that the practice is the result of the growing awareness of the position of Augustus and not of any kind of direction is clear from the fact that the practice gradually becomes more common towards the end of Augustus' reign. (Crawford 1985, 273).

And it should be observed that the civil wars marked a turning-point in this too, with portrait-coins struck by and under the auspices of the leading Roman participants (Crawford 1985, 275). It has been claimed that Pompey's features are visible on the head which appears on a coin of Aristarchus, dynast of Colchis, but the identification remains at best uncertain (Golenko 1974 presents the various arguments).

Throughout, the impact of local tradition is apparent. To build cities and to name them after oneself or a member of the ruling dynasty was a commonplace of hellenistic kingship. Under the Principate kings continued to name such cities after themselves and members of their families, but, at the same time, they adapted their traditional practice to include the other 'rulers' of their kingdoms—the emperor and the imperial family. Similarly, titular formulations on the pattern of 'friend of' (in Greek, *phil(o)-*) were traditional in royal hellenistic titulature—e.g.*philadelphus* ('friend of his brother', or 'brother-loving'), *philopator* ('father-loving') etc. These traditional titles continued to be used but the tradition was broadened to take in first 'friend of Rome' (*philorhomaeus*) and then 'friend of Caesar [i.e.the emperor]' (*philocaesar*) and the like. And, of course, the terminology of friendship was also familiar within Roman society, so that, for example, 'friend of Caesar' (Latin, *amicus Caesaris*) was a term in use at Rome itself.

The expression and acknowledgment of authority through religion and coinage were similarly traditional, especially, perhaps, in the East, but also in the West, where our evidence does not allow us to trace changes and continuities with any great confidence.

Suetonius' general observations on the changes which occurred under Augustus are especially valuable because they confirm impressions given by other sources which would by themselves be open to some question. Josephus provides a wealth of evidence on the Herods and their relationships with the imperial family. However, he says little of royal Jewish relations with Republican Rome, largely it seems, because there was little to say. Therefore, Josephus can tell us little about the impact of the change from Republic to Principate upon the rulers of Judaea. Moreover, it is always possible that the Herods were atypical. Judaism evidently made them atypical in one sense: the imperial cult, for example, could hardly be introduced in Jerusalem, though it might be ventured in a Greek city like Caesarea-Strato's Tower.

Strabo's evidence might also be questioned. In the last sentence of his geography of the Roman world, completed in the reign of Tiberius, he states:

> And kings too and dynasts and decarchies are and have always
> been in the emperor's part of the empire. (Strabo 17 p.840).

Strabo's account of the administrative division of the empire, according to which some parts were allocated to the emperor and others to the Roman people (hence, the Senate), is over-schematic. Quite apart from errors of detail, Strabo does not make it clear that in practice the emperor was involved in the affairs of 'senatorial' provinces and that he came to issue detailed instructions (*mandata*) to governors of such provinces (Levick 1985, 7-11 with the Introduction to this volume). Nevertheless, though Strabo may be over-schematic and may indeed underestimate the role of the emperor, there is no reason to doubt his assertion that kings were the particular domain of the emperor, especially since Josephus, Suetonius and others support it. We have already observed Tacitus' explicit complaint on this very point (*Ann.* 3.55).

Under the Republic no king had the Roman citizenship as far as we know. By the end of Augustus' reign most friendly kings had it, though in most cases it was seldom included in their titulature. For most, their kingship was evidently much more important than their possession of Roman citizenship, unless, it seems, they were dealing with a Roman community. It can be no simple chance that a large percentage of our scant evidence on the tenure of Roman citizenship by kings is derived from inscriptions in Latin produced in essentially Roman communities, like Gades in Spain and Heliopolis in Syria (Braund 1984, 39-53). The rulers of the Crimean Bosporus are, once again, exceptional, for they regularly give their full Roman citizenship nomenclature in Greek in their own inscriptions in their kingdoms. But for most kings Roman citizenship, though sometimes significant, was often not so. After all, kings maintained, as they had always done, relationships with cities other than Rome, in the course of which they tended to collect citizenships. In addition, there were many very ordinary Romans who could boast Roman citizenship, but who will have seemed to kings, no doubt, to be persons of little account: kings would not have been proud to share the status of such Romans.

However, although its long-term significance may not have been entirely apparent even to the kings themselves, the possession of Roman citizenship made kings more a part of Roman society than they had been under the Republic. As an act of beneficence by the emperor it was also part of his patronage. It is no surprise that, as Suetonius states, kings appeared before Augustus in their togas, material indications of their citizenship. They had assumed their Roman and Augustan identities. And in later years, it was the possession of Roman citizenship that made it possible for royalty to enter the Senate: an early and striking case is King Alexander of Cilicia, who rose to become consul before AD 109 (Braund 1984, 180n.81).

Unfortunately, our information on awards of citizenship to kings is so scant that we cannot be sure when such an award was first made. The first award may have been made by Caesar. And there is good reason to believe that Antony awarded citizenship to his friend Polemo, whom he made Polemo I of Pontus (Braund 1984, 41-2). Moreover, if, as seems likely, Herod had shared in Caesar's grant of citizenship to his father, he would have already been a Roman citizen when Antony and Octavian had him made king of Judaea in 40 BC (Schürer 1973, 271): though Josephus says nothing of it, Herod may have been the first Roman citizen-king. At the same time, if Caesar or Antony gave Roman citizenship to royalty then one of them may well have awarded citizenship to Cleopatra of Egypt, remarkable as that may seem. Antony's supposed will, under which Cleopatra was said to inherit, is only credible if Cleopatra was a citizen, for only a citizen

could inherit under Roman law (cf.Crook 1957). Whether Antony really
made such a will or whether Octavian invented it, it had nevertheless to
be credible (Braund 1984, 179). We should not be surprised if Octavian's
regime preferred to describe her not as a citizen but as a deadly foreign foe.
If Antony and his version of history had won at Actium, we would no doubt
have heard much more of Octavian's dealings with the royalty of Thrace
and his 'plan' to marry a Thracian princess, while Julia married the bride's
royal father (Suet.*Aug.*63.2).

Under the Principate kings were now indeed much more a part of the Roman
empire. The possession of citizenship by kings may well have been more a
symptom than a cause of their greater integration and acceptance within
the Roman empire. In the Late Republic it had become more common for
Roman citizenship to be bestowed upon non-Romans, but never upon kings.
Under the Republic the notion that a king might also be a Roman citizen
(and thus, that a Roman citizen might be a king) may well have seemed
unacceptable or simply inappropriate. However, with the establishment of
the Principate a political shift had occurred at Rome which perhaps made a
king's tenure of Roman citizenship a little more tolerable, although it could
only sit most uneasily with the ideology of a restored Republic. It may
well be that the innovation had been eased by the rise to kingship of men
who already possessed Roman citizenship—men like Herod and Polemo.
However that may be, kings now proclaimed—in their building, coinage,
names, titles and behaviour—their participation in the Roman empire of
the Principate.

The integration of kings had been greatly facilitated by the shift from Republic to Principate. Relationships between Republican Rome and the
kings had been mediated and sometimes undermined by complex personal
relationships between competing Romans and, often, between competing
kings. Thus Cicero describes himself as being at odds with Clodius, with
their respective friends, King Deiotarus and King Brogitarus, on either
side, themselves at odds in Galatia (*Har.Resp.*29). The two disputes were
thoroughly intertwined. By contrast, under the Principate, state-patronage
and personal patronage were focussed together upon the emperor and his
family before all others. Kings could now afford to commit themselves
demonstrably to a particular patronage—imperial patronage. Amid the

shifting political sands of the Republic, the wise king needed to keep open as wide a circle of patronage as possible, though he might become especially connected with particular individuals and groupings. Thus Deiotarus was connected not only with Cicero but also with Pompey, Atticus, Caesar and others. Deiotarus' connections thus included four of the key figures of the Late Republic. When Pompey and Caesar went to war Deiotarus had claims on him from both sides: Caesar was later to complain that the king had chosen to support Pompey and not him (*Bell.Alex.*67-8).

The complexity and shifting nature of Roman politics under the Republic probably explains the fact that even Pompey did not have a city named after him by a client king. The history of royal will-making points in the same direction. Under the Republic kings made wills wherein they left their kingdoms to the Roman people and called upon the Roman people to be the guardian of their heirs (Braund 1984, 129-64). But it was only under the Principate that particular individual Romans, namely the emperor and members of his family, were named as royal heirs—as when, for example, Prasutagus of the Iceni left part of his kingdom to Nero (*Ann.* 14.61). Salome, sister of Herod, bequeathed estates to Livia, who seems to have played a large part in relations with royalty, especially perhaps with queens (Jos.*AJ* 18.31; Purcell 1986 provides a broader context). Under the Principate, as Suetonius tells us, it was Augustus who appointed guardians where necessary, as in the case of Archelaus of Cappadocia, who is said to have suffered temporary mental illness (Dio 57.17).

Augustus had turned client kings into an arm of government which was connected especially closely to himself and his family, incorporating power and prestige. Antony, again, must take some credit, for his arrangements in the East, actual and projected, had shown the way: Augustus left most of Antony's actual arrangements in place (Bowersock 1965). And, of course, Antony in turn had built upon Republican practice: members of the Republican elite had traditionally exercised patronage over kings—a few, like Scipio Aemilianus and Pompey, had done so on a considerable scale. Many of Augustus' activities can best be understood as the traditional activities of a member of the Roman Republican elite functioning on a higher and wider plane. So, in large measure, his dealings with kings: in exercising personal patronage over kings Augustus was behaving in traditional fashion. But there was a crucial difference, of course: Augustus was pre-eminent and thus tended to usurp the position of the state with regard to kings as in much else. From the kings' point of view the Roman imperial family was hardly distinguishable from another royal dynasty—even under the Republic Romans had commonly been conceived of as royal personages by non-Romans (Richardson 1979; Millar 1984, 3).

Continuity in the effective operation of this arm of government was promoted by the up-bringing of royal offspring at Rome with the imperial family. It was something of a tradition in the hellenistic world to send sons abroad for their 'education'. Under the Republic, one or two young royals had spent substantial periods in Rome, but short visits were more common. Antony had collected many royal offspring at Alexandria. Augustus took over many of these children and with them the practice. Once again, royal tradition coincided with Augustus' interests; Antony is again to the fore, again building on Republican precedent—notably that of Sertorius in Spain (Braund 1984, 9-21).

The financial problems of, respectively, Ptolemy XII Auletes of Egypt and the future Agrippa I of Judaea illustrate the realities of the change from Republic to Principate. When Auletes needed money he contracted a multiplicity of debts with large numbers of creditors, including Rabirius Postumus. He used this money to win the favour and support of leading Romans, such as Pompey and Caesar (who were also his creditors). This was all the more necessary since his case was at the centre of political in-fighting within the Republican elite (Wiseman 1985a, ch.3). By contrast, Agrippa borrowed large sums within the imperial household, exploiting the contacts he had formed there in his youth, and from members and close connections of his own family. This money he spent freely in order to gain the favour of the future emperor Gaius and important imperial freedmen (Braund 1984, 59-63). Under Republic and Principate alike kings had to borrow and spend in order to establish, increase and protect bonds of pa-tronage, but under the Principate the game was played on different, more restricted ground. In striving for Roman patronage under the Republic, the king was forced to deal with a large number of Romans of varying disposi-tion towards each other. Under the Principate they had to deal primarily with the emperor, his family and those with access to and influence with them. We can now understand why Claudius' freedman Narcissus was feted by kings (Dio 60.34.4; cf. Millar 1977, 72). Another freedman of Claudius, M.Antonius Pallas, had pretentions to royalty in his own right by descent from the ancient royalty of Arcadia (and thus, indeed, of Rome itself) - pretentions which were even acknowledged publicly in a senatorial decree (Tac.*Ann.*12.53). Pallas' brother, Antonius Felix, as procurator of Judaea, married into the Herodian dynasty: he is said to have married three queens in total (Suet.*Claud.*28 with Braund 1984, 178n.79).

Agrippa's case indicates the value of the connections that could be formed during a youth spent at Rome. Young royals presumably also gained a better understanding of Roman society and of the Latin language. If Agrippa did indeed, as Josephus describes, play a key role in negotiations between Claudius and the Senate after the assassination of Gaius, then he will certainly have needed all the knowledge he had gained in his youth. Agrippa was able to mediate effectively because he was both an outsider and an insider within the Roman elite (Jos.*AJ* 19.236ff.).

The benefits of an up-bringing at Rome accrued similarly to young royals who were in Rome as *obsides*, a term which we can only translate, imperfectly, as 'hostages'. None were ever held to account for their family's actions and they seem to have enjoyed extensive freedom at Rome. And, of course, any young royal in Rome could in theory be used as a hostage, though no cases are attested. In fact, it is sometimes hard to know whether a young royal was in Rome as a 'hostage' or not. A case in point are the sons of Phraates IV of Parthia, who came to Rome with their families after Augustus' agreement with the king in 20 BC. The *Res Gestae* proclaim that Phraates sent his sons and grandsons to Rome as pledges of friendship (*RG* 32.2). Their arrival redounded to the emperor's credit. For that reason Augustus displayed them at a public spectacle by leading them across the arena and seating them behind himself (Suet.*Aug*.43.4). Moreover, Augustus could claim still further credit by sending Phraates' son, Vonones, to be king of Parthia at Parthian request (*RG* 33; cf.Suet.*Aug*.21.3).

Indeed the 'giving' of kings to kingdoms and vice-versa was adjudged a significant expression of the emperor's power and beneficence (e.g. Sen.*De Clem*. 1.1). The high status of kingship made the appointment and creation of a king an act of outstanding greatness. Hence, the great ceremonies held by emperors and members of the imperial family, at Rome and abroad, in which kingdoms and kingship were formally bestowed. Most famous— but less exceptional than is sometimes imagined— is Nero's bestowal of the kingdom of Armenia upon Tiridates in AD 66 (Braund 1984, 27, citing precedents, e.g. Suet.*Claud*.25). It is therefore no surprise to find Roman emperors issuing coins proclaiming that kings have been 'given' to kingdoms—*REX...DATUS*—and depicting themselves doing just that (Göbl 1961). When Arrian wrote to Hadrian, describing the situation on the eastern coast of the Black Sea, he took care to state which emperor had given kingdoms to the various local rulers: this was not simply an account of cold fact—it was also a statement of imperial greatness (Arr.*Periplus* 11; cf.also Appian *Preface* 7).

To receive embassies from distant kings or to offer refuge to kings in flight from their kingdoms was to add still further to imperial prestige— hence the place of these activities among Augustus' achievements (*RG* 31-

32). In fact the attitude and behaviour of kings towards an emperor was taken very much into account when judgments were made about an emperor's worth (SHA *Ant.Pius* 9.10; cf. Suet.*Nero* 57.2). Quite simply, dealing with kings wa's a substantial part of the emperor's job—even a preoccupation. When Augustus died he left legacies to kings (Dio 56.32.2); according to the *Historia Augusta*, when Antoninus Pius died his last words were 'about the state and those kings with whom he was angry' (SHA *Ant.Pius* 12.7).

However, for all the special connections between kings and the imperial family, kings also came into contact with other Romans: to that extent there was a certain continuity from Republic into Principate, despite Tacitus' complaints to the contrary (*Ann.* 3.55; cf.Saller 1983). In particular, Roman magistrates in the provinces were very likely to encounter royalty, under Republic and Principate alike. When a Roman general advanced into hostile territory he met not only hostile forces, who might be led by kings, but also royalty prepared to accept his friendship to achieve their own ends.

An inscription dedicated by Gaius Cornelius Gallus, first prefect of Egypt, states that when he had subdued the troublesome area of southern Egypt known as the Thebaid:

> ...envoys of the king of the Ethiopians were given audience at Philae and that king was received into protection, and a ruler of the Ethiopian Triakontaschoinos was established. (*ILS* 8995).

We may compare an inscription which records the career of Ti. Plautius Silvanus Aelianus and, in particular, gives details of his dealings with kings and others when he was governor of Moesia under Nero:

> ...he brought across more than 100,000 Transdanubians for the payment of taxes, together with their wives and children and leaders or kings...; kings previously unknown or hostile to the Roman people he brought across to the bank he protected so that they might pay reverence to the Roman standards; he returned to the kings of the Bastarnae and Roxolani their sons, to those of the Dacians, their brothers, captured or seized from enemies; from some of them he received hostages; by these actions he confirmed and advanced the peace of the province, the king of the Scythians having also been removed from the siege of Chersonesus, beyond the Borysthenes. (*ILS* 986).

As Agricola moved north through Britain, the flight to him of an Irish king prompted thoughts of an invasion of Ireland:

> Agricola had received one of the kinglets of the Irish who had been driven out by an uprising at home. He kept him in the name of friendship until the time was ripe. (Tac.*Agr.* 24.3).

Evidently Agricola hoped to use this kinglet as part of a conquest and subsequent administration of Ireland: no doubt the kinglet would have been happy in the role, as was, it seems, Cogidubnus in Britain (Tac.*Agr.* 14). Invasions of Britain itself had been prefaced by the flight of disgruntled British royalty to the Roman invader. A Trinovantian princeling, Mandubracius, had fled to Caesar in Gaul (Caes.*BG* 5.20) and Adminius had taken refuge with Gaius, poised to invade Britain (Suet.*Cal.*44.2) ; Claudius had similar dealings with estranged Britons (Dio 60.19.1). Tacitus' observations on Maroboduus at Ravenna make it quite clear that he understood the value to Roman diplomacy of an ousted ruler (*Ann.*2.63; see above). Augustus may have made diplomatic use of the British royalty that fled to him (*RG* 32); they would no doubt have played their part in any Augustan invasion of Britain.

It cannot be stressed sufficiently, however, that dealings with royalty were very much a regular feature of a Roman governor's period of office. Such contacts were by no means confined simply to grand exploits like those of Gallus, Silvanus and Agricola. It is striking that wherever we have substantial information about a governor's period of office, there too we find him involved with royalty. Verres, as governor of Sicily, dined with a Syrian prince who was on his way home from Italy: according to Cicero Verres robbed the prince of a splendid dedication which had been intended for Capitoline Jupiter (Cic.*In Verr.*2.4.67). In his speech against Piso, Cicero alleges that, as governor of Macedonia, he took a bribe from a Thracian ruler to kill a chieftain of the Bessi (*In Pis.*84). As governor of Syria in 55 BC, Gabinius restored Ptolemy Auletes to his throne in Egypt, again, it is said, at a price (Cic.*Rab.Post.*21 with Braund 1984, 60). Cicero's provincial correspondence tells in detail of his close relationship with Deiotarus of Galatia—how his son stayed with the king, how the king helped him to extract monies from another king (Ariobarzanes III of Cappadocia) and, above all, how the king's forces were much stronger than his own and thus vital to the defence of the area in the event of a Parthian invasion. Cicero had, unusually, also been given the task, while governor of Cilicia, of safeguarding the position of King Ariobarzanes in Cappadocia. And we hear how Cicero received letters from kings further east, reporting on the activities of the Parthians (see, conveniently, Treggiari 1972).

Under the Principate Josephus shows in detail the complex relationships between the Roman governors of Syria and Judaea, the numerous members of the Herodian dynasty and the rulers of Nabataea. The New Testament confirms the situation in outline: we are told how Pilate and the tetrarch Herod Antipas passed Jesus to and fro. It has been suggested that Pilate was particularly concerned to ingratiate himself with Antipas (Hoehner 1972, 182). As governor of Bithynia-Pontus, Pliny had to deal with the kingdom of the Crimean Bosporus (Pliny *Epp*.10.63; 67). We have already noted Arrian's dealings with kings during his governorships of Cappadocia.

For their part, kings enjoyed relationships with civic communities situated within Roman provincial territory. Under the Principate the royals of Mauretania were given public office (presumably, honorary) in Roman colonies in Spain—at Gades and New Carthage. King Sohaemus of Emesa and Agrippa II held similar offices in the Roman colony at Heliopolis (Baalbek). Athens was packed with royal dedications which continued to be made there from the hellenistic period through the Roman empire. Athens in particular was the show-case of the Mediterranean world where not only kings but also leading Romans and others made dedications (Braund 1984, 75-90). This provides part of the context for the projected royal completion of the temple of Olympian Zeus at Athens discussed above (Suet.*Aug*.60). Such activities also help to put into context royal dedications on the Capitol at Rome. Such dedications were the application to Rome, caused by the sheer importance of Rome, of long-standing royal practice.

Within his kingdom the king was left essentially to his own devices, to rule largely as he would have done were he completely independent. The laws and traditions of the kingdom continued. Yet certain broad and rather ill-defined requirements were demanded by Rome of a king. Most importantly he must maintain order within his kingdom. Augustus seems to have required that Archelaus restore order in Judaea by a cautious use of his power as ethnarch: Archelaus' failure to do so led to his removal by Augustus in AD 6 (Jos.*AJ* 17.342-3). Complaints had been lodged against

Archelaus by his enemies in Judaea. It was vital for the ruler to maintain good strong relationships with those influential at Rome, the centre of power, precisely in order to survive such complaints. So much is true of Republic and Principate alike.

Powerful connections at Rome were no less important for the ruler, should he enter into dispute with a local Roman official. When Agrippa I of Judaea fell out with Marsus, the Roman governor of Syria, the king sought to use his friendship with the emperor Claudius to harm Marsus. In the end, Agrippa had some success, but Marsus' accusations of revolt were too grave and plausible to be ignored by the emperor. Agrippa had made his kingdom militarily stronger and had hosted a gathering of eastern kings at Tiberias (Jos.*AJ* 19.326-63). Both were to the advantage of Rome and the emperor. Had not Augustus promoted the coming-together of kings? Yet such activities made an accusation of revolt all too easy, for, of course, they also facilitated actual revolt, as with the kings who gathered in Vespasian's cause (above).

Alternatively, disputes between a king and a Roman official might be dealt with locally: the king could call upon the aid of a neighbouring well-disposed governor to support him. Thus, Varus, governor of Syria, was called in by Archelaus to protect the property of Herod from the imperial procurator, Sabinus (Jos.*AJ* 17.221-2).

The king was expected, in particular, to control piracy and banditry in and around his kingdom. The Piracy Law of 101/100 BC specifically instructs the consul to write to the kings of Cyprus, Egypt, Cyrene and Syria:

> ...to make clear that it is also right that they should take action to prevent any pirate from using as a base of operations their kingdom, land or territories and that no officials or garrison-commanders appointed by them should harbour the pirates and to take action, as far as is in their power, that the Roman people shall have in them zealous contributors to the safety of all... (Hassall *et al.* 1974, 207).

In the late third century BC the Illyrian Wars had been caused, in part, by Queen Teuta of Illyria's inability or unwillingness to control the piracy that was central to her subjects' way of life (Dell 1967; cf.Braund 1984, 92). Roman concern to suppress piracy may well have prompted moves in 75 BC to take back the coastal *ager publicus* ('public land') held by Hiempsal II of Numidia (Cic.*de leg.agr.* 2.58). The idea that it is the job of kings to put down pirates is taken for granted by Cicero (Cic.*In Verr.*2.4.66-67; *pro Flacco* 30). Under the Principate, Zenodorus was removed from his principality in the mountains of Trachonitis, specifically because he had not

only —in a situation akin to that of Teuta in Illyria (Jos.*AJ* 16.271-1)
failed to control banditry, but had, it was said, actively encouraged bandit-
raids by his subjects upon Damascus (Jos.*AJ* 15.344). The Polemonid rulers
of Pontus maintained a fleet which was engaged in suppressing the endemic
piracy of the Black Sea with the help of other local rulers. It may have
been in the course of action against pirates that the prefect of that fleet,
Anicetus, formed or consolidated friendship with a kinglet of the Caucasian
coast (Tac.*Hist.*3.47-8). The scale of endemic piracy in the Caucasus helps
to explain why Rome preferred to use kings there: with reference to Cilicia
Tracheia, Strabo suggests that large-scale piracy and banditry might lead
Rome to prefer royal rule:

> Since the area was naturally suited to acts of piracy by land
> and by sea...it was decided that these places should be placed
> under royal rule rather than under Roman governors with
> judicial functions, who would not always be on the spot and
> would not have troops. (Strabo 14 p.671).

Strabo's point is clear enough—the presence of many bandits suggests, even
requires, the operation of kings. That is not at all to say of course that
Roman forces were incapable of suppressing banditry: they might even be
called in to help a king to do just that (Tac.*Ann.*6.42.6). What is less clear
is how far Strabo is correct to impute this line of thought to those who made
decisions at Rome, of whom he was not one; yet the other evidence cited
tends to bear out his imputation. Interestingly, Strabo hints elsewhere
at dissatisfaction with the efforts of Roman governors—by contrast with
kings—in dealing with pirates (11. p.496; though kings could also prove
unsatisfactory, cf.Strabo 14. pp.668-9).

It is not always immediately obvious that a particular occurrence or
measure relates to the maintenance of local order. When Claudius ordered
his edict ensuring Jewish rights to be posted by kings and dynasts as well
as in Italy and the provinces, he was including monarchies in measures
designed to forestall the all-too-common conflict between Jew and non-
Jew. This edict was about religion but it was also very much about security
and order (Jos.*AJ* 19.287-91 with Rajak 1984). We should note in passing
the role of Jewish monarchs in this edict, using their close friendship with
Claudius to attain their ends. Small wonder that Claudius was said to
have been insulted by a Greek anti-Semite as being 'the cast-off son of
Salome the Jewess' (Smallwood 1967, no.436). The Julio-Claudians and
the Herods were intimately—though, it seems, not that intimately—related
from Caesar and Augustus onwards.

The maintenance of order and suppression of banditry and piracy was
part of the frontier role of client kings. Client kingdoms commonly were the

frontier, not least because Rome needed to evolve a relationship with areas adjoining the territories which she administered directly. To ask whether they were inside or outside the empire is essentially to miss the reality of the situation—the question is a conundrum created by legal theorists wrestling with the finer points of *postliminium*, by which a Roman citizen technically lost his citizenship when he left the empire and regained it upon his return within it (Cimma 1976). In practice, the frontier was not a line but a region. As part of that region a kingdom tended to be seen as part of the empire. Client kingdoms have often been regarded as buffers, protecting Rome against attack from foreign enemies. To a large extent this view is correct— we have seen Deiotarus' role in the defence of the eastern frontier in Cicero's day. An inscription from the reign of Gaius describes certain kings as 'the bodyguards of the empire' and provides vivid insights into the matrix of beneficence and cult within which kings, cities and emperors operated (Smallwood 1967, no.401). But the concept of the buffer-state must be refined. Although Romans occasionally display cynicism in the exploitation of royal forces (e.g. Tac.*Ann*.14.23.4), they much more commonly and importantly stress the notion that kings and kingdoms are under Roman protection (e.g. Caes.*BG* 1.44: Tac.*Ann*.4.5). Cicero even describes Rome as the 'citadel of kings and foreign nations' (*pro Sulla* 33). And we have seen already how Augustus claimed to protect kings. Rome needed to maintain this ideology of protection. That ideology could only be a major factor in deterring attacks upon allies and in attracting new alliances. Allies might on occasion be abandoned to hostile forces, but never lightly. Kings and Rome were engaged in mutual protection and fought together in campaigns of defence and aggression to mutual advantage. Throughout, the resources of kingdoms were crucial—armed forces (often specialists), supplies, money, strategic positions, local knowledge and contacts and more besides. This was their contribution to the empire. They paid no regular direct taxes, though they were required to make *ad hoc* payments on demand. Under the Republic in particular defeated kings (and cities) were often required to pay fixed sums, often in annual stages over a fixed period of years, which were sometimes described as war-indemnities, but which had a distinct air of retribution.

Kingdoms were much more than the term 'buffers' might suggest. Indeed, in the fourth century AD Julian is said to have regarded the very suggestion that kingdoms were buffers protecting Rome as an insult to the honour of the Roman state: Rome should be the protector not the protected (Amm.Marc.23.2.1). Moreover, kings performed functions on the frontier which the buffer-notion tends to hide. In particular, kings were also intermediaries. As such they had dealings both with Rome and with potential enemies of Rome, like Izates of Adiabene, who sent some of his sons to Claudius to be 'hostages' at Rome and the rest to Parthia (Jos.*AJ* 20.37). Yet, though valuable to Roman interests, the intermediary position of the king made him vulnerable to Roman suspicions of treachery. Where a Roman campaign failed, client kings were convenient scapegoats.

The use of client kings was a successful means of imperial administration because kings too gained much from their relationships with Rome. Many owed their very thrones to Rome, as did Herod, who had no dynastic claims to rule in Judaea (Jos.*AJ* 14.386ff.). In his *Gallic War* Caesar tells us how he settled succession disputes with the result that several Gallic rulers owed their positions to him. Under the Principate in particular, Rome seems to have exercised considerable control over succession to the throne in the various kingdoms: it was apparently as a special privilege that Augustus granted Herod the right of appointing his own successor to the throne of Judaea, a privilege of which Herod seems not to have dared to take full advantage (Jos.*AJ* 16.128 with Braund 1984, 26). Kings could expect Roman support against threats to their positions from within their kingdom as well as outside. Garrisons might even be installed, like the forces Gabinius left in Egypt to support Auletes. Of course, such support might not be forthcoming, especially if a ruler was held responsible for his own plight (like Archelaus in AD 6) and/or if forces hostile to the king took care to come to an arrangement with Rome (Tac.*Ann.* 12. 29-30). Ultimately, the ruler's position might not be tenable, even with active Roman backing. In Britain in AD 69 Cartimandua, queen of the Brigantes, was forced to flee, despite Roman military intervention to support her (Tac.*Hist.*3.45; cf.*Ann.*12.40). It is impossible accurately to assess the extent to which the king's association with Rome forestalled threats to his position before they had even manifested themselves. In any event, whether the king was given Roman military support or not he might at least expect Rome to provide a refuge. And, as we have seen, to offer refuge to a king would bring the emperor prestige and a potentially useful tool of diplomacy (Tac.*Ann.*2.63).

Rome might extend the kingdoms of her friends, as she extended the kingdom of Pergamum after the Treaty of Apamea (188/7 BC) (Hansen 1971, 92ff.; cf. for an example in the first century AD, Tac.*Ann.*14.26). Kings might also receive gifts redolent of Roman power, notably the trappings of high office at Rome such as the curule chair (Braund 1984, 27-29). Kings might also gain financially: Augustus had Herod oversee mining on Cyprus and allowed the king to keep half the proceeds (Jos.*AJ* 16.128).

Direct financial gifts or payments to kings are often called subsidies by modern scholars. There is no evidence for the payment of regular subsidies to kings under the Republic—perhaps a further indication of the looser nature of their bond with Rome at that time. Under the Principate, by contrast, subsidies became a significant factor in Roman imperial strategy, praised or condemned by our sources largely in accordance with their broader assessments of the worth of the emperor who bestowed them. A detailed survey of the evidence on subsidies indicates the efficiency and minimal cost of subsidies as a means of frontier influence, control and defence (Gordon 1948).

The receipt of subsidies can only have bolstered the king's position within his kingdom. And the king's friendship with Rome could bring other economic advantages. Tacitus tells us of the special trade privileges with the Roman empire which were enjoyed by the Hermunduri of Germany (Tac. *Germ*.41). Maroboduus' capital contained traders attracted from the Roman empire, it seems, by a trade agreement (Tac. *Ann*.2.62). The right of trade (*ius commercii*) was a standard tool of Roman diplomacy from at least the fifth century BC into the Late Empire. Trade and friendship with Rome and Romans were especially significant in times of special local need. Herod used his friendship with Rome and the prefect of Egypt to gain Egyptian grain under preferential treatment. This grain he distributed to his subjects in Judaea, who were suffering severe famine. In that way Herod, whose reign had not been popular hitherto, made himself very popular indeed. The benefits to Herod of his links with Rome and Romans are clear. Worthy of particular attention is the fact that Herod distributed some of this grain in the Roman province of Syria, where, in consequence, he also became extremely popular (Jos. *AJ* 15.299-316). Once more the interrelationships between Roman officials, provinces and kingdoms become apparent.

The success of Rome as an imperial power depended in large part upon her ability to gain and maintain royal friends. The bestowal of benefits upon these royal friends was central to that ambition and, at the same time, such beneficence coincided with the beneficial ideology of Rome in general and the emperor in particular (cf.Millar 1977). We have seen how the change from Republic to Principate further secured and co-ordinated the bond between kings and Rome. Rome made no attempt to smooth out the significant differences that obtained from kingdom to kingdom: even to attempt it would have been to put at risk the entire stability of the system. Nothing was to be gained by such interference, save more work and problems for Roman government. A broad formulation—at its fullest, *rex et socius atque amicus* ('king and ally and friend': Tac.*Ann*.4.26), or more commonly some briefer variant—was applied to rulers of many different kinds in the West as well as in the East. Of course, Romans were aware of local differences and were sometimes led to employ particular titles in particular situations—in Judaea, Archelaus was made ethnarch, not king, in AD 6, partly, at least, out of respect for Jewish tradition and as a sop to those Jews who opposed his appointment altogether. And we hear of tetrarchs, like Antipas; minor rulers are often called kinglets (*reguli*) and dynasts. But when Romans considered their empire as a whole, local details were not permitted to obfuscate the picture. 'The kings' and 'the kingdoms' are given a regular and prominent place whenever the Romans discussed their empire, as for example in Tacitus' famous review of its scope which gives a prominent place to 'the allied kings' (*socii reges* ; *Ann*.4.4ff.). Such generalized terminology did not denote a precise juridical category and was strictly inaccurate, as is usual with generalizations, but it did constitute a convenient, working category—even for legal theorists. Particularly convenient, since it corresponded to conceptions of monarchy rooted deep in Roman ideology: 'the king' had an important place in Roman thought as far back as we can trace it, not least because of the importance of the kings of early Rome to the ideology of the Republic and the Principate thereafter. By contrast, ethnarchs, tetrarchs, kinglets and dynasts were essentially foreign to Roman categories of social and political thought. For that reason, this variety of titles was all the more easily and conveniently subsumed under the notion of the king.

At Rome, 'king' was a title redolent of power, authority, status and wealth—exotic and attractive, yet potentially dangerous. As we have seen, the associations of kingship in Roman thought were by no means entirely negative: it is worth remembering that in the Roman past there were bad kings like Tarquinius Superbus, but there were also good kings like Servius Tullius. From the non-Roman standpoint, especially in the East, Romans could be thought of as kings (Millar 1984, 3). In many respects there was a certain similarity between kings and leading Romans, not least a shared high status. That similarity, together with an increasing familiarity with kings at Rome, helps to account for the osmosis which occurred between kings and the Roman elite, so that by the second century AD a king could become a senator (consul, even) and a senator could become a king (Braund 1984, 172-4). Under the Empire marriage between Romans of the elite and royalty became, first, feasible and, by the Late Empire, unproblematic. Brunt puts it very well:

> From Trajan onwards most emperors came from the provinces

> and the eternal city celebrated its millennium in AD 247 un-
> der the rule of an Arab sheikh. (Brunt 1964-5, 274).

Thereafter, the fall of the empire in the West might better be conceived as a further stage in this osmotic process, when a king became emperor—and, indeed, an emperor who might be seen as a client king of the emperor in the East (cf.Jones 1974, ch.19 with Pabst 1987).

Abbreviations

AE   *L'Année Epigraphique* (in progress).

IGRR   R.Cagnat, *Inscriptiones Graecae ad Res Romanas Pertinentes* (1911-27).

CIG   *Corpus Inscriptionum Graecarum.*

CIL   *Corpus Inscriptionum Latinarum.*

EJ   V.Ehrenberg and A.H.M.Jones, *Documents illustrating the reigns of Augustus and Tiberius* (2nd.edn., 1955 and repr.with additions, 1976).

I.Eph.   *Die Inschriften von Ephesos = Inschr.ften griechischer Städte aus Kleinasien* (in progress).

ILS   H.Dessau, *Inscriptiones Latinae Selectae* (1892-1916).

IRT   J.M.Reynolds and J.B.Ward-Perkins, *Inscriptions of Roman Tripolitania* (1951).

MAMA   *Monumenta Asiae Minoris Antiqua.*

MW   M.McCrum and A.G.Woodhead, *Documents of the Flavian Emperors* (1961).

NSRC   A. Maiuri, *Nuova silloge epigrafica di Rodi e Cos* (1925).

OGIS   W.Dittenberger, *Orientis Graeci Inscriptiones Selectae* (1903-5).

RDGE   R.K.Sherk, *Roman Documents from the Greek East* (1969).

SEG   *Supplementum Epigraphicum Graecum* (in progress).

Syll 3.   W.Dittenberger, *Sylloge Inscriptionum Graecarum* (3rd. edition, 1915–24).

Bibliography

Abbott, F.F., and Johnson, A.C. 1926, *Municipal Administration in the Roman Empire*, Princeton.

Adam, T. 1970, *Clementia Principis*, Stuttgart.

Alfoldy, G. 1974, *Noricum*, London.

Applebaum, S. 1964, Jewish status at Cyrene in the Roman period, *Parola del Passato* 19. 291-303.

Badian, E. 1972, *Publicans and Sinners*, Oxford.

Baldini, A. 1978, Discendenti a Roma da Zenobia ?, *Zeitschrift für Papyrologie und Epigraphik* 30. 145-9.

Balsdon, J.P.V.D. 1979, *Romans and Aliens*, London.

Barrett, A.A. 1979, The career of Tiberius Claudius Cogidubnus, *Britannia* 10. 227-42.

Bernhardt, R. 1985, *Polis und römische Herrschaft in der späten Republik (149-31 v.Chr.)*, Berlin-New York.

Birley, A.R. 1966, *Marcus Aurelius*, London.

Birley, A.R. 1971, *Septimius Severus*, London.

Blagg, T.F.C. 1984, An examination of the connexions between military and civilian architecture, in Blagg and King 1984, 249-63.

Blagg, T.F.C. and King, A.C. 1984, *Military and civilian in Roman Britain*, Oxford.

Bogaers, J.E. 1979, King Cogidubnus in Chichester: another reading of *RIB* 91, *Britannia* 10. 243-54.

Boon, G.C. 1974, *Silchester: the Roman town of Calleva*, Newton Abbot.

Bowersock, G.W. 1965, *Augustus and the Greek World*, Oxford.

Bowersock, G.W. 1969, *Greek Sophists in the Roman Empire*, Oxford.

Bowersock, G.W. 1984, Augustus and the East : the problem of the succession, in F.Millar and E.Segal (eds.), *Caesar Augustus*, Oxford, 169-88.

Bowie, E.L. 1970, Review of B.Levick *Roman Colonies in Southern Asia Minor, Journal of Roman Studies* 60. 202-7.

Bowman, A.K. and Thomas, J.D. 1983, *Vindolanda: the Latin writing-tablets*, London.

Braund, D.C. 1980, The Aedui, Troy and the Apocolocyntosis, *Classical Quarterly* 30. 420-25.

Braund, D.C. 1984, *Rome and the Friendly King : the character of client kingship*, London-New York.

Braund, D.C. 1985, The social and economic context of the Roman annexation of Cyrenaica, in G.Barker, J.Lloyd and J.Reynolds (eds.), *Cyrenaica in Antiquity*, Oxford, 319–25.

Braund, D.C. 1987, The legacy of the Republic, in J.Wacher (ed.), *The Roman World*, London, 55-68.

Braund, D.C. 1988, Function and dysfunction : personal patronage in Roman imperialism, in A.F.Wallace-Hadrill (ed.), *Patronage in Ancient Society*, London, forthcoming.

Broughton, T.R.S. 1938, Roman Asia Minor, in T.Frank (ed.), *An Economic Survey of Ancient Rome*, Baltimore, 4. 499-916.

Brunt, P.A. 1961, Charges of provincial maladministration under the Early Principate, *Historia* 10. 189-223.

Brunt, P.A. 1964-5, Reflections on British and Roman imperialism, *Comparative Studies in Society and History* 7. 267-88.

Brunt, P.A. 1971, *Italian Manpower, 225 BC-AD 14*, Oxford.

Brunt, P.A. 1975, Stoicism and the Principate, *Papers of the British School at Rome* 43. 7-35.

Brunt, P.A. 1978, *Laus imperii*, in P.Garnsey and C.R.Whittaker (eds.), *Imperialism in the Ancient World*, Cambridge, 159-91.

Burnham, B.H. 1986, The origins of Romano-British small towns, *Oxford Journal of Archaeology* 5.2. 185-203.

Burton, G.P. 1975, Proconsuls, assizes and the administration of justice under the Empire, *Journal of Roman Studies* 65. 92-106.

Burton, G.P. 1987, Government and the provinces, in J.Wacher (ed.), *The Roman World*, London, 423-39.

Castrén P. 1975, *Ordo Populusque Pompeianus; policy and society in Roman Pompeii*, Rome.

Chaniotis, A. 1985, Eine neue lateinische Ehreninschrift aus Knossos, *Zeitschrift für Papyrologie und Epigraphik* 58. 182-7.

Chastagnol, A. 1981, L'inscription constantinienne d'Orcistus, *Mélanges d' Archéologie et d'Histoire de l'Ecole Française de Rome* 93. 381-416.

Cimma, M.R. 1976, *Reges socii et amici populi Romani*, Milan.

Collis, J. 1984, *Oppida: earliest towns north of the Alps*, Sheffield.

Cotton, M.A. 1979, *The Late-Republican Villa at Posto, Francolise*, British School at Rome.

Cotton, M.A. 1985, *The San Rocco Villa at Francolise*, British School at Rome.

Crawford, M.H. 1985, *Coinage and Money under the Roman Republic*, London.

Crook, J.A. 1957, A legal point about Mark Antony's will, *Journal of Roman Studies* 47. 36-8.

Cunliffe, B. 1976, The origins of urbanisation in Britain, in Cunliffe and Rowley 1976, 135-161.

Cunliffe, B. and Rowley, T. (eds.) 1976, *Oppida in barbarian Europe*, Oxford.

Dejevsky, N. 1980, The urbanisation of Eastern Europe, in A. Sherratt (ed.), *The Cambridge Encyclopaedia of Archaeology*, 314-18.

Dell, H.J. 1967, The origin and nature of Illyrian piracy, *Historia* 16. 344-58.

Dorandi, T. 1985, Der "gute König" bei Philodem und die Rede des Maecenas vor Octavian (Cassius Dio 52.14-40), *Klio* 67. 56-60.

Drinkwater, J.F. 1983, *Roman Gaul : the Three Provinces 58 B.C.-A.D. 206*, London.

Drinkwater, J.F. 1985, Urbanisation in the Three Gauls: some observations, in Grew and Hobley 1985, 49-55.

Duncan-Jones, R.P. 1982, *The Economy of the Roman Empire*, 2nd.edn., Cambridge.

Duncan-Jones, R.P. 1985, Who paid for public buildings in Roman cities?, in Grew and Hobley 1985, 28-33.

Eckstein, A.M. 1980, *Unicum subsidium populi Romani* : Hiero II and Rome, 263-215 BC, *Chiron* 10. 183-203.

Etienne, R. 1974, *La Vie Quotidienne à Pompeii*, Paris.

Fentress, E.W.B. 1979, *Numidia and the Roman army*, Oxford.

Fishwisk, D., and Shaw, B.D. 1976, Ptolemy of Mauretania and the conspiracy of Gaetulicus, *Historia* 25. 491-4.

Franklin, J.L. 1980, *Pompeii; the Electoral Programmata, Campaigns and Politics A.D.71-79*, American Academy at Rome.

Fraser, P. (inc.note by S.Applebaum) 1950, Hadrian and Cyrene, *Journal of Roman Studies* 40. 77-90.

Frere, S.S. 1972, *Verulamium excavations I*, London.

Garnsey, P. 1970, *Social Status and Legal Privilege in the Roman empire*, Oxford.

Garnsey, P. 1974, Aspects of the decline of the urban aristocracy in the empire, *Aufstieg und Niedergang der römischen Welt* II.1 229-52.

Garnsey, P., and Saller, R. 1982, *The Early Principate*, Greece and Rome, new surveys in the Classics no.15, Oxford.

Garnsey, P., and Saller, R. 1987, *The Roman Empire: economy, society and culture*, London.

Göbl, R. 1961, REX...DATUS. Ein Kapitel von der Interpretation numismatischer Zeugnisse und ihren Grundlagen, *Rheinisches Museum* 104. 70-80.

Golenko, K. 1974, Aristarchus of Colchis and his coins, *Vestnik Drevnei Istorii* 4. 105-10 (in Russian).

Goody, J. (ed.) 1966, *Succession to High Office*, Cambridge.

Gonzalez, J. 1986, The lex Irnitana : a new copy of the Flavian municipal law, *Journal of Roman Studies* 76 147- 243.

Gordon, C.D. 1948, *The subsidization of border peoples as a Roman policy in imperial defence*, Diss., Michigan.

Grew, F. and Hobley, B. 1985, *Roman urban topography in Britain and the western Empire*, London.

Groenman van Waateringe, W. 1980, Urbanisation and the north-west frontier of the Roman Empire, in W.S. Hanson and L.J.F. Keppie (eds.), *Roman Frontier Studies 1979*, Oxford.

Hall, A.S. 1979, Who was Diogenes of Oenoanda ?, *Journal of Hellenic Studies* 49. 160-3.

Hansen E.V. 1971, *The Attalids of Pergamon*, 2nd.edn., Ithaca, New York.

Hanson, W.S. 1987, *Agricola and the conquest of the north*, London.

Harris, W.V. 1979, *War and Imperialism in Republican Rome, 327-70 BC*, Oxford.

Hassall, M.W.C., and Tomlin, R.S.O. 1979, Inscriptions, *Britannia* 10. 339-56.

Hoehner, H.W. 1972, *Herod Antipas*, Cambridge.

Hopkins, K. 1978, Economic growth and towns in classical antiquity, in D.Abrams and E.A.Wrigley (eds.), *Towns and Societies*, Cambridge, 35-77.

Hopkins, K. 1983, *Death and renewal*, Cambridge.

Horsfall, N. 1985, *CIL* VI 37965 = *CLE* 1988 (epitaph of Allia Potestas), *Zeitschrift für Papyrologie und Epigraphik* 61. 251-72

Jashemski, W.F. 1979, *The Gardens of Pompeii, Herculaneum and the villas destroyed by Vesuvius*, New York.

Jones, A.H.M. 1940, *The Greek City*, Oxford.

Jones, A.H.M. 1971, *The Cities of the Eastern Roman Provinces*, 2nd.edn., Oxford.

Jones, A.H.M., 1974, *The Roman Economy*, (ed.) P.A.Brunt, Oxford.

Jones, C.P. 1971, The Levy at Thespiae under Marcus Aurelius, *Greek, Roman and Byzantine Studies* 12. 45-8.

Kennedy, D.L. 1987, The East, in J.Wacher (ed.), *The Roman World*, London, 266-308.

Keppie, L. 1984, *The Making of the Roman Army*, London.

Levick, B. 1967, *Roman Colonies in Southern Asia Minor*, Oxford.

Levick, B. 1985, *The Government of the Roman Empire: A Sourcebook*, London.

Lintott, A.W. 1978, The Capitoline dedications to Jupiter and the Roman people, *Zeitschrift für Papyrologie und Epigraphik* 30. 137-44.

Lintott, A.W. 1981, What was the "imperium Romanum" ?, *Greece and Rome* 28. 53-67.

McCrum, M., and Woodhead, A.G. 1961, *Documents of the Flavian Emperors*, Cambridge.

Macinnes, L. 1984, Brochs and the Roman occupation of Lowland Scotland, *Proc.Soc.Antiq.Scot.* 114. 235-49.

Macinnes, L. 1988, Iron Age society in south-east Scotland: the archaeological potential, in J.C. Barrett *et al.* (eds.), *The barbarian peoples of northern Europe*, Oxford.

Mackie, N. 1983a, *Local administration in Roman Spain AD 14-212*, Oxford.

Mackie, N. 1983b, Augustan colonies in Mauretania, *Historia* 32. 332-58.

Macmullen, R. 1974, *Roman Social Relations*, New Haven.

Macmullen, R. 1982, The epigraphic habit in the Roman empire, *American Journal of Philology* 103. 223-46.

Macmullen, R. 1959, Roman imperial building in the provinces, *Harvard Stud. Class. Phil.* 64. 207-35.

Macurdy, G.H. 1937, *Vassal Queens*, Baltimore.

Maddoli, G. 1963-4, Le Cretule del Nomophylakeion di Cirene, *Annuario della Scuola Archeologica di Atene* 41-2. 39-145.

Magie, D. 1950, *Roman Rule in Asia Minor*, Princeton.

Meiggs, R. 1973, *Roman Ostia*, 2nd.edn., Oxford.

Millar, F.G.B. 1968, Local cultures in the Roman empire : Libyan, Punic and Latin in Roman Africa, *Journal of Roman Studies* 58. 126-51.

Millar, F.G.B. 1977, *The Emperor in the Roman world*, London.

Millar, F.G.B. 1982, Emperors, frontiers and foreign relations, *Britannia* 13. 1-23.

Millar, F.G.B. 1984, The political character of the classical Roman Republic, *Journal of Roman Studies* 74. 1–19.

Millar, F.G.B. 1987, Empire, community and culture in the Roman Near East: Greeks, Syrians, Jews and Arabs, *Journal of Jewish Studies* 38. 143-64.

Millett, M. 1984, Forts and the origins of towns: cause or effect?, in Blagg and King 1984. 65-74.

Mocsy, A. 1957, Zur Geschichte der peregrinen Gemeinden in Pannonien, *Historia* 6. 488-98.

Nash, D. 1976, The growth of urban society in France, in Cunliffe and Rowley 1976, 95-133.

North, J.A. 1981, The development of Roman imperialism, *Journal of Roman Studies* 71. 1-9.

Nussbaum, M. 1986, *The Fragility of Goodness: luck and ethics in Greek tragedy and philosophy*, Cambridge.

Nutton, V. 1971, Two Notes on Immunities, *Journal of Roman Studies* 61. 52-63.

Nutton, V. 1978. The beneficial ideology, in P.Garnsey and C.R.Whittaker (eds.), *Imperialism in the Ancient World*, Cambridge, 209-21.

Oliver, J.H. 1941, *The Sacred Gerusia*, Hesperia, Supplement 6.

Pabst, A. 1986, *Divisio Regni: Der Zerfall des Imperium Romanum in der Sicht der Zeitgenossen*, Bonn.

Peacock, D.P.S. 1982, *Pottery in the Roman world : an ethno-archaeological approach*, London.

Pleket, H.W. 1981, A free *demosios, Zeitschrift für Papyrologie und Epigraphik* 42. 167-70.

Pleket, H.W. 1984, City elites and economic activities in the Greek part of the Roman empire: some preliminary remarks, *Acts of the Eighth International Congress of Greek and Latin Epigraphy, Athens 1982*, 103-4.

Price, S.R.F. 1984, *Rituals and Power: the Roman Imperial Cult in Asia Minor.* Cambridge.

Purcell, N. 1986, Livia and the womanhood of Rome, *Proceedings of the Cambridge Philological Society* 32. 78-105.

Rajak, T. 1984, Was there a Roman charter for the Jews ?, *Journal of Roman Studies* 74. 107-23.

Rawson, E. 1975, Caesar's heritage : hellenistic kings and their Roman equals, *Journal of Roman Studies* 65. 148-59.

Reynolds, J.M. 1959, Four Inscriptions from Roman Cyrene, *Journal of Roman Studies* 49. 95-101.

Reynolds, J.M. 1982a, *Aphrodisias and Rome*, Society for the Promotion of Roman Studies, London.

Reynolds, J.M. 1982b, Senators from Crete and Cyrene, in S.Panciera (ed.), *Epigrafia e Ordine Senatorio*, Rome, 677-83.

Reynolds, J.M., and Goodchild, R.G. 1965, The City-lands of Apollonia in Cyrenaica, *Libya Antiqua* 2. 103-7.

Reynolds, J.M., Beard, M., and Roueché, C. 1986, Roman Inscriptions 1981-5, *Journal of Roman Studies* 76. 124-45.

Reynolds, J.M., and Tannenbaum, R.F. 1986, *Jews and Godfearers at Aphrodisias*, Cambridge Philological Society.

Rich, J.W. 1988, Patronage in inter-state relations, in A.F.Wallace-Hadrill (ed.),*Patronage in Ancient Society*, London, forthcoming.

Richardson, J.S. 1976, *Roman Provincial Administration*, repr.1984.

Richardson, J.S. 1979, Polybius' view of the Roman empire, *Papers of the British School at Rome* 47. 1-11.

Richardson, J.S. 1986, *Hispaniae: Spain and the Development of Roman Imperialism, 218-82 BC*, Cambridge.

Richardson J.S. 1987, The purpose of the Lex Calpurnia de repetundis, *Journal of Roman Studies* 77. 1-12.

Rivet, A.L.F. 1977, The origins of cities in Roman Britain, in P.M. Duval and Frézouls, E. (eds.), *Thèmes de recherche sur les villes antiques de l'occident*, Paris, 161-72.

Roueché, C. 1984, Acclamations in the Later Roman Empire, *Journal of Roman Studies* 74. 181-99.

Russell, D.A., and Wilson, N.G. (eds.) 1981, *Menander Rhetor*, Oxford.

Saller, R.P. 1983, *Personal Patronage under the Early Empire*, Cambridge.

Schindler, F. 1972, *Die Inschriften von Bubon, Nord-Lykien*, Wien.

Schürer, E. 1973, *The History of the Jewish People in the Age of Jesus Christ (175 BC-AD 135)*, (eds.) G.Vermes and F.Millar, Edinburgh.

Shaw, B.D. 1984, Bandits in the Roman empire, *Past and Present* 105. 3-52.

Sherwin-White, A.N. 1966, *The Letters of Pliny*, Oxford.

Sherwin-White, A.N. 1973, *The Roman Citizenship*, 2nd.edn., Oxford.

Sherwin-White, A.N. 1984, *Roman Foreign Policy in the East*, London.

Sherwin-White, S.M. 1975, A Coan Domain in Cyprus, *Journal of Hellenic Studies* 95. 182-4.

Smallwood, E.M. 1967, *Documents illustrating the reigns of Gaius, Claudius and Nero*, Cambridge.

Smith, M.F. 1978, Fifty-five fragments of Diogenes of Oenoanda, *Ancient Society* 28. 39-92.

Smith, M.F. 1979, Eight fragments of Diogenes of Oenoanda, *Ancient Society* 29. 69-89.

Smith, R.M., and Porcher, E.A. 1964, *A History of the Recent Discoveries at Cyrene* (with catalogue of inscriptions pp. 109-17).

Souris, G. 1982, The Size of Provincial Embassies to the Emperor under the Principate, *Zeitschrift für Papyrologie und Epigraphik* 48. 235-44.

Stevenson, G.H. 1949, *Roman Provincial Administration till the age of the Antonines*, Oxford.

Swan, V.G. 1975, Oare reconsidered and the origins of Savernake ware in Wiltshire, *Britannia* 6. 37-61.

Syme, R. 1939, *The Roman Revolution*, Oxford.

Syme, R. 1981, Rival cities, notably Tarraco and Barcino, *Ktema* 6. 27-185.

Talbert, R.J.A. 1980, Pliny the younger as governor of Bithynia-Pontus, in C.Deroux (ed.), *Studies in Latin Literature and Roman History*, Brussels, 2. 412-35.

Treggiari, S. (ed.) 1972, *Cicero's Cilician Letters*, LACTOR 10.

Van Berchem, D. 1983, Une inscription flavienne du musée d'Antioche, *Museum Helveticum* 40. 185-96.

Versnel, H.S. 1970, *Triumphus*, Leiden.

Wacher, J. 1974, *The towns of Roman Britain*, London.

Wacher, J. 1987, *The Roman Empire*, London.

Walbank, F.W. 1981, *The Hellenistic World*, London.

Walthew, C.V. 1975, Town house and villa house in Roman Britain, *Britannia* 6. 189-205.

Waltzing, J.F. 1895, *Etude historique sur les corporations professionelles chez les Romains*, Paris.

Ward Perkins, J.B. 1970, From Republic to Empire; reflections on the early provincial architecture of the Roman West, *Journal of Roman Studies* 60. 1-19.

Webster, G.A. 1966, Fort and town in early Roman Britain, in J.S. Wacher (ed.), *The civitas capitals of Roman Britain*, Leicester, 31-45.

Welles, C.B. 1934, *Royal Correspondence in the Hellenistic Period*, London.

Wightman, E.M. 1977, Military arrangements, native settlements, and related developments in early Roman Gaul, *Helinium* 17. 105-26.

Wightman, E.M. 1985, *Gallia Belgica*, London.

Wilkes, J.J. 1969, *Dalmatia*, London.

Wiseman T.P. 1971, *New Men in the Roman Senate (139 BC-AD 14)*, Oxford.

Wiseman T.P. 1985a, *Catullus and his World*, Cambridge.

Wiseman, T.P. 1985b, *Roman Political Life (90 BC-AD 68)*, Exeter.

Wörrle, M. 1987, Polis et chora à Oenoanda de Cibyratide, in E.Frézouls (ed.), *Sociétés urbaines, sociétés rurales dans l'Asie Mineure et la Syrie hellénistique et romaine*, Strasbourg.

NOTES ON CONTRIBUTORS

David C. Braund teaches in the Department of Classics, Exeter University. His research specialises in the frontier areas of the Roman empire, especially in the Black Sea region. His publications include *Rome and the Friendly King: the character of client kingship* (1984).

W.S. Hanson teaches in the Department of Archaeology at Glasgow University. He specialises in the Roman frontier in Britain, and his publications include *Agricola and the conquest of the north*, 1987.

Joyce Reynolds, FBA, is a Fellow of Newnham College, Cambridge. She specialises in the study of inscriptions from the Roman empire, particularly those of Turkey and Cyrenaica. Her publications include *Aphrodisias and Rome* (1982).

EXETER STUDIES IN HISTORY
General Editor: Jonathan Barry

Other paperbacks in this series include:

No. 7 *Roman Political Life, 90BC–AD69*
    edited by T.P. Wiseman
    1985, 88 pp.
    ISBN 0 85989 225 5

No. 20 *Roman Public Buildings*
    edited by I.M. Barton
    1989, 190 pp., illustrated
    ISBN 0 85989 239 5

No. 23 *Satire and Society in Ancient Rome*
    edited by Susan H. Braund
    1989, 160 pp.
    ISBN 0 85989 331 6 X

No. 30 *Death of an Emperor: Flavius Josephus*
    edited with an introduction and commentary
    by T.P. Wiseman
    1991, 140 pp.
    ISBN 0 85989 356 1